2-21-75

THE
PUERTO RICAN
EXPERIENCE

THE PUERTO RICAN EXPERIENCE

See last pages of this volume
for a complete list of titles

THE PUERTO RICAN PRESS REACTION
TO THE UNITED STATES, 1888-1898

PAUL NELSON CHILES

ARNO PRESS

A New York Times Company

New York — 1975

Reprint Edition 1975 by Arno Press Inc.

Reprinted from a copy in
  The University of Illinois Library

The Puerto Rican Experience
ISBN for complete set: 0-405-06210-9
See last pages of this volume for titles.

Manufactured in the United States of America

———◆———

Library of Congress Cataloging in Publication Data

Chiles, Paul Nelson, 1910-
    The Puerto Rican press reaction to the United States,
1888-1898.

    (The Puerto Rican experience)
    Originally presented as the author's thesis, Univer-
sity of Pennsylvania, 1942.
    Bibliography: p.
    1. Press--Puerto Rico. 2. Puerto Rico--Politics
and government--To 1898. 3. Puerto Rico--Relations
(general) with the United States. 4. United States--
Relations (general) with Puerto Rico. I. Title.
II. Series.
PN4944.C5 1975   079'.7295   74-14225
ISBN 0-405-06215-X

UNIVERSITY OF PENNSYLVANIA

THE PUERTO RICAN PRESS REACTION
TO THE UNITED STATES, 1888-1898

A DISSERTATION

IN HISTORY

PRESENTED TO THE FACULTY OF THE GRADUATE SCHOOL IN
PARTIAL FULFILLMENT OF THE REQUIREMENTS FOR
THE DEGREE OF DOCTOR OF PHILOSOPHY

PAUL NELSON CHILES

PHILADELPHIA

1944

ACKNOWLEDGMENTS

The writer has been assisted by important criticisms and suggestions from a number of historians, colleagues, and friends. Throughout the period of the project Professor William E. Lingelbach, former Dean of The College, University of Pennsylvania, was a constant source of inspiration and guidance. Among the colleagues and historians who have given assistance in the preparation of parts of the manuscript are: Dona Pilar Barbosa de Rosario, Professor Lidio Cruz Monclova, and Professor Rafael W. Ramirez of the University of Puerto Rico, and Dr. Arthur Watts and Dr. John La Monte of the University of Pennsylvania History Department. The writer is indebted to Don Luis Caballer and Don Emilio J. Pasarell for the use of their fine private newspaper collections, to the Carnegie Library, San Juan, P. R., and to the Periodical Library of the University of Puerto Rico. Miss Margarita Walsh, Librarian of the latter collection, is especially remembered for her kind cooperation at all times. The files of "La Democracia" and "La Correspondencia de Puerto Rico" were thrown open to this historical research, for which courtesy the writer is greatly indebted. The writer wishes to thank the following students of the University of Puerto Rico for aiding in this work: George T. Bothwell, Ignacio Cortes, Rafael Lomba, Angel Arce, George Fernandez Ramos and Rafael Velazquez Munoz.

This dissertation is dedicated to my wife, who has been a loyal helper without whose criticism, proof-reading, and sacrifice the work would have never been completed.

PAUL N. CHILES.

Contents

Due to the exigencies of the war emergency the following chapters have been omitted: Chapter III. Attitude toward the United States and Yankees in General; Chapter IV. Prominent Americans as Seen Through Puerto Rican Eyes; VIII. American Education; IX. American Morals, Religion, and "Blue Laws". These chapters may be consulted in the Graduate School office of the University of Pennsylvania.

Introduction

The American influence upon Puerto Rico is far different from that upon such a sister nation as England. When two nations with a common racial, linguistic, and cultural background meet and exchange views various results ensue. England and the United States have a great deal in common, much more than pronounced Anglophobes admit. The influence exerted by a Mother Country upon a daughter nation is an accepted fact but the opposite relationship has received slight attention.* Naturally the older nation would view the younger with a certain condecension characteristic of an elder relative, the younger would be considered presumptuous in daring to think of influencing the other, and the relationship would assume the friendly animosity of cousins. However, in spite of that rather strained atmosphere, the United States did influence England in many respects. American slang, industrial achievements, movies, education, and newspapers were among the many factors that affected British life and did much to make Englishmen speak of the "American Peril".** The American influence upon a people with a radically different racial history, religion, culture, and language was naturally very different from the American Impact upon England. There is one marked difference between the attitude of Puerto Ricans and Englishmen toward American influence.

Dr. Heindel states that admiration for things American cut across party lines. This was not the case in Puerto Rico because Puerto Ricans were essentially 'party-men' in their attitude toward the "Colossus of the North". The conservatives followed the dictates of the Peninsula*** and had absolutely no use for anything American except the American dollar; the liberals, on the other hand, were eager and willing to learn from the United States. Between these two groups there was a wide gulf which was impossible to bridge when the subject of the United States arose. The American Impact on England, on the other hand, was not an impact that followed strictly political lines. This development was impossible because, for one reason, the United States was not regarded as a dangerous enemy which had designs upon British colonies. Nor was there that mercurial and explosive Latin temperament involved in the relations between England and the United States as there was between the United States and Spain. The Puerto Rican press reaction to the Northern Republic is characterized by comedy, drama, and even pathos but that upon England seems to have the cold mutton quality.

Dr. Heindel points out that by 1895 the American press was superior in its technical achievements to the British and that the British learned from American methods. The same is true of Puerto Rico. There are other instances where England and Puerto Rico had similar opinions of the United States. Interest in American crime and sex life was high; the distorted comments on American liquor laws prove that American drinking restrictions were just simply not understood; the American appeal to rights and ideals was seen as so much hypocrisy; co-education and women suffrage received critical treatment; and the expression "There is no culture in the United States" issued from both England and Puerto Rico.

* The best work so far on this subject has been that of Dr. Richard Heathcote Heindel, The American Impact on Great Britain, 1898-1914. (Philadelphia, 1940)
** Dr. Heindel states that this term is usually applied to American economic dangers.
*** The Peninsula is a term commonly applied to Spain by Latin-Americans.

The cultural influence, then, appears only in isolated articles because by and large, Puerto Ricans continued to believe that the United States was a land of the buffalo, Indians, pioneers, gold-miners, and backwoodsmen. It was recognized that there was an industrialized East because of the great number of manufactures imported to Puerto Rico. However, that wealthy section of the United States where culture could thrive was considered completely mercenary in outlook, with little or no time for the finer arts. Culture, it was believed, was non-existent in the United States.

Dr. Heindel has stated that little good was printed in the English press about the United States; this was not true in Puerto Rico because there the liberal Puerto Rican press was consistently favorable to the United States and even the conservatives printed some friendly articles, especially at times like the Columbian Exposition. There was no boom at any time in American speakers in Puerto Rico because the natural course for Puerto Rican societies to follow was to employ lecturers of their own race. Tourism is essentially a product of the twentieth century in the island and even yet has reached no great importance. The United States exerted no profound or revolutionary political effect upon England, but the American influence on Puerto Rican political thought was marked. Naturally this followed party lines. The liberals looked to the United States for guidance and copied American institutions and governmental theories as is attested by the great amount of conservative denunciation. The conservatives ever regarded the Westward Movement in the United States as a sign that American imperialism would later take a southward turn.

Mr. Emilio J. Pasarell in his study on the origin and development of the Puerto Rican theater has found an early instance of theatrical relations between the United States and Puerto Rico. William Pearman, who had been the favorite in New York City for many seasons, came to Puerto Rico and was one of the first artists to sing at the San Juan Municipal Theater.[1] However, in spite of Pearman's success in the island, the practice of bringing theatrical talent from the United States was not continued. As a result the American influence on the Puerto Rican stage and theater had a very slight development.

Social customs and family relationships were not affected until the coming of the Americans after 1898. Old World procedure characterized Puerto Rican society and family life. The male was the lord and master of his household and the woman's place was in the home and the church. The dueña ruled in all her glory and even today occupies a strong position in Puerto Rican social life.

Puerto Rican styles and dress came from Spain and France during the period 1888-1898. Puerto Rico was essentially an Old World country in that respect and did not want to become Americanized. The change, however, is apparent after 1898. On the other hand, there was an admiration and a respect for American scientific achievements. Puerto Ricans who had studied medicine and dentistry in the United States were proud to put out a shingle that said 'American Dentist' or 'American Doctor'. It showed that they had learned the hard way and it also helped their business.

The writer had devoted a great deal of space to the political aspects of the American influence. The economic, political, educational, and governmental phases of this influence are largely interpreted in terms of politics

---

1/Pasarell, Emilio J.: Origen y Desarrollo de las Representaciones Teatrales en Puerto Rico (Compilacion Cronologica) MSS.

to the apparent exclusion of any other influence. This is explained by the fact that the Latin is primarily a political creature. He thinks, eats, and discusses politics from the time he learns to talk to the time he dies. The Latin high school and college student is vitally interested in the devious machinations of the politicians and in what is going on in the Capitolio. This is greatly in contrast with the average American student who glances at the headlines, reads the comics, and then turns to the sport page. Politics to him mean campus politics. The affairs of Senators and Congressmen mean little or nothing in his young life. He will vote when he is twenty-one, if he thinks about it. The Latin is completely different. Any student in the University of Puerto Rico is a walking encyclopedia of political names, policies, and history. That is true today and was equally true of the youth during the period 1888-1898.

Puerto Rico's geographic position in the Antilles has always bade it a coveted island in the ever strategic Caribbean area, from the free-booting days of the Spanish Main to the era of Yankee hegemony. This fact was recognized by the Spanish queen who wryly remarked that the walls of El Morro Castle must be made of gold, since they cost the Crown so much treasure. That Lord Cumberland, Drake, and the Dutch admiral, Bodoin Henry all had more or less the same idea is evidenced by the fact that they tried, unsuccessfully, to seize the island. El Morro and its sister fortress, San Cristóbal, (both are located in San Juan) defeated all efforts made by enemy nations until 1898 to capture this lesser Pearl of the Antilles. Naturally, Cuba, with its greater size and more central location in the Gulf of Mexico, had far greater attraction to imperialistic nations before the twentieth century. The harbor of Habana, the proximity of the island to the gold of Mexico and the produce of the Mississippi Valley, as well as the size of the Greater Antille, made it the main prize with the result that Puerto Rico was shoved, undeservedly, into the background. Although Cuba occupied the center of the stage and was counted the choicest morsel of Spain's colonial empire in the Gulf, the strategists of the Peninsula and the enemy generals (Drake, Bodoin Henry, et al) well knew the strategic possibilities of Puerto Rico. The home government poured money into the seemingly insatiable maw of Puerto Rican defense needs until El Morro Castle was made into the second most complex fortification of the Western Hemisphere, inferior only to Cartagena, Columbia. The impregnability of the island was well demonstrated by the number of sieges that it withstood in the course of its history in spite of the fact that better known places such as Habana received most of the credit for a successful resistance.

Geography placed Puerto Rico on the well known 'hot-spot' both under Spain and under the United States. Occupying as it does the right angle position of the chain of islands that begins with Cuba and extends down to the coast of South America, Puerto Rico has always been the exposed point of the Antilles. It is the easternmost of the Greater Antilles and is the pivot island where the chain of islands breaks sharply southward toward South America. This fact was appreciated by the Spaniards and is tardily being appreciated by the Americans today.

Puerto Rico under the Americans occupied no great position of importance until World War II. During the first World War, when Allied navies had more of an upper hand than in 1941, Puerto Rico's defense of the Caribbean area was restricted to a native infantry regiment and a 'disappearing' cannon. The latter's chief claim to fame was its one-shot performance during the war when a German ship that had been interned tried to leave port. The gun was fired; it promptly turned over backwards and was immobilized for the duration of the war. However, the German captain thought that the cannon was truly a disappearing type and returned to port rather than face another artillery shell. Such was Puerto Rico's part in Caribbean warfare in 1917. Let it be said, however, that the island contributed her full share of men and money to the American war effort of that conflict.

During the uncertain years that followed the Treaty of Versailles, Puerto Rico was left very much to itself until the United States decided upon an 'all-out' defense effort in 1940. In spite of the indifference with which Puerto Rico had been treated by Congress since World War I, there were many people who viewed the island in a far different light. There were those who felt that Puerto Rico should serve as a Spanish-American cultural center and become the 'Bridge of the Americas'. The island, due to its geographic position, could easily fulfill that function and develop into an intellectual crossroads for Spanish and Anglo-Saxon America. Thus the American influence upon Puerto Rico which had been so evident in the island long before 1898 would spread throughout the Americas in a far more effective way than through the present over-worked Good Will missions. This type of influence, aided and directed by a Pan-American University located in Puerto Rico would be, in the opinion of the writer, an intelligent step in the direction of hemisphere solidarity and the Good Neighbor policy.

Those of the military of the Billy Mitchell type saw in Puerto Rico an admirable defense base. The island, in their eyes, was about to return to its position of military importance which it had held during the hey-day of the Spanish colonial empire. Defense, with the advent of the airplane, greatly increased its effective range. The defense of Uncle Sam's back-door no longer depended on shore batteries with a maximum range of fifty miles. The airplane revolutionized American defense and the United States' first line of defense now lay in the Antilles. An invader could be met by planes based in the Antilles and also in bases located on the bulge of Brazil. When this plan is worked out the Gulf of Mexico will be America's Mare nostrum and the Panama Canal will be safe. Puerto Rico's part in this scheme is simple. It is the only island whose facilities can be fully exploited by the United States. In that way the defense of the Gulf depends greatly upon Puerto Rican air-fields and naval bases, both of which make it the key of American defense in the Caribbean.

The Puerto Rican Press

A study of the "Puerto Rican Press Reaction to the United States" is impossible without a brief survey of journalism in Puerto Rico. There is some doubt as to the exact date of the introduction of the press into Puerto Rico as some authorities place it at 1806, 1807, or 1808. Which of these dates is correct is immaterial to this study; suffice it to say that one of those dates is correct and that the history of the island's press began early in the nineteenth century. Puerto Rico was far behind Cuba (where the first press was introduced in 1723) and the other Spanish colonies, where it first made its appearance early in the sixteenth century. The delay in Puerto Rico has been ascribed by the late Dr. Antonio S. Pedreira[1] to the island's insularism or provincialism which is still a factor to be considered in its political development.

In the main, there are three periods in Puerto Rican history. They are: (1) From the discovery and conquest of 1808; (2) 1808 to 1898, which has been called the "Golden Age" of Puerto Rico; (3) From 1898 on or the Period of Indecision. This last period bears its name because the island has been virtually at the crossroads since the American Invasion, undecided whether to remain belligerently Spanish or to embark upon a path of American democracy colored by the Spanish heritage. It is true that Spanish remains and will probably always remain the dominant language, that bi-lingualism has fallen far short of the expectations of the American governors, and that Spanish culture remains the ideal and the real in spite of the American occupation. However, it must be remembered that Spain's influence dates back to four hundred years of continuous development, whereas the American is little more than forty years old.

1808, when Napoleon invaded Spain, marked the beginning of a period of liberal relations between Spain and the colonies. The Spaniards who undertook to drive out Napoleon recognized the political rights of the American colonials and felt that if the Spanish empire were to be saved it could only be saved through the co-operation of the Mother Country and its children. As a result American deputies were elected to the Junta Suprema Central where equality was decreed between Spaniards and colonials. In general, then, a liberal period was inaugurated between Spain and the colonies with this co-operation.

However, with the return of Ferdinand VII to absolutism, the empire began a period of disintegration which ceased in 1826, by which time Spain had lost everything in America with the exception of the Antilles. During the time of the South American revolutions Cuba and Puerto Rico was the refuge for all Peninsulares who were escaping the persecution of the nationalist generals. Bolivar expressed South American sentiment in his cry "Death to the Spaniards". As a result of the Spanish loyalist influx into the Antilles public opinion there became more and more that of a conservative or 'incondicional' character. The period 1808-1837, * then, was one of political integration for Cuba and Puerto Rico while the opposite tendency prevailed elsewhere in the Spanish colonies.

The year 1808 had a further meaning for Puerto Rico. By that time the era of the foundation, organization, and exploitation of the colony had

---

* 1837, the date when the Puerto Rican deputies were expelled from the Spanish Cortes.

ended and a period more definitely Puerto Rican was about to begin. This was further emphasized by the introduction of the first press c. 1808 and the development of insular journalism during the Golden Age of the nineteenth century. There are five well defined periods of Puerto Rican journalism, each differentiated from the other by events of high political importance. The first extends from the foundation c. 1808 of the first Puerto Rican paper, La Gaceta de Puerto Rico which was a governmental organ, to 1870, when the effects of the Spanish Revolution of 1868 were first felt in the island. The second, 1870-1875, is known as the period of liberalism, when Peninsular liberalism was reflected in Puerto Rico. The third, 1875-1890, was a recession, viewed in the light of the stirring years, 1870-1875; the liberal period for Puerto Rico ended in 1875 and conservatism was the order of the day until 1890 when a reorganization of politics and journalism took place as a result of the effects of the Componte.* The fourth period, 1890-1898, was as important as that of 1870-1875 because the Spanish authorities were fighting a losing battle against the insular liberals in spite of censorship, fines, and the hundreds of other vexing devices than an autocratic government could invent and use. The period after 1898, that of the American occupation, is the great age of Puerto Rican liberalism. It is the one in which the liberals have come into their own and have exploited their good fortune to the utmost, founding papers with almost reckless abandon.

Political events and the founding of newspapers were inseparable in significance. The Spanish government itself was responsible for the first newspaper, La Gaceta de Puerto Rico, which the writer called "the first Puerto Rican paper" but which, in reality, was a Spanish paper that reflected the views of the government, gave brief notices of insular and European news, and had the heavy and dry reading characteristic of governmental literature. Until 1839 the Gaceta was the only paper deserving of the name of newspaper. In that year the Boletín Instructivo y Mercantil de Puerto Rico was founded. With the founding of the Boletín, the Gaceta confined itself more and more to governmental dispatches, military orders, and royal decrees while the Boletín operated mainly in the field of Journalism. It is probable that the founding of the Boletín was closely connected with the Decree of 1837, which expelled the Puerto Rican deputies from the Spanish Cortes and ordered that the island was to be governed in the future by special laws. As a result there were no newspapermen, politicians, orators, or writers who could express publically the ideas of the Puerto Rican people. If anyone was so foolhardy as to do so, he immediately experienced the heavy hand of Spanish authority. Therefore, it is not too much to say that the foundation of the Boletín was permitted so that the government could point out to the dissident spirits that Spain allowed its colony to "express itself". This paper speedily became the semi-official organ of the Spanish government and was always alligned on the side of authority. Consequently, it was not a Puerto Rican paper; it was Spanish. From the date of its foundation, 1839, to 1868, the date of the Spanish Revolution, it had no opposition in Puerto Rico. It towered head and shoulders over any liberal paper that was foolish enough to defy the government.

Spanish liberalism by means of revolution succeeded in 1868 but Puerto Rican liberalism (by that means failed in that year with "El Grito

---

* The Componte, 1887, was a period of extreme reaction and oppression in Puerto Rico.

de Lares".* Puerto Rico was asked to send deputies to the Spanish Cortes after the successful Spanish revolution of 1868. The deputies went to Spain in 1870. This date marked the beginning of political parties in Puerto Rico and also the first flowering of Puerto Rican journalism. The press with its political papers directed affairs and struggled to keep the island abreast of world liberalism. It gave encouragement to the Cortes of 1872-1873, which tried to liberalize the colonial regime. However, liberalism was doomed with the overthrow of the liberal government in 1873, and Puerto Rico returned to a conservative system in 1875 (again two years behind the march of events in the Peninsula).

The next political event which specifically changed the course of Puerto Rican journalism was the Componte of 1887. The word "componte" comes from the verb "componer" which means 'behave'; "componte", then, is the imperative form meaning "behave yourself"; it is a Puerto Rican provincialism used to designate the year of extreme reaction, 1887. Now, of course, it is applied to any period of governmental autocracy and high-handedness. This reaction was caused by the Constitutional Assembly of the Autonomist Party in March of 1887, which was immediately denounced in violent terms by the 'incondicionales'. The term 'incondicionales' was applied to those Puerto Ricans who unconditionally attached themselves to the cause of Spain in Puerto Rico. It was the boast of the Boletín that it was 'The organ of the Spaniards without conditions'; in other words it meant 'Spain, right or wrong' and Puerto Rico second. The governor was General Romualdo Palacio, a man open to 'reason' from the conservative point of view. Therefore, the 'incondicionales' took him to Aibonito, a small hill-town, where they persuaded him that the liberals were anti-Spanish and ipso facto enemies of the government. Then began the black page of the Spanish administration in Puerto Rico. Liberals were persecuted, imprisoned, and tortured during this counter-revolution staged by the reactionaries. Almost all of the liberal papers of the island were either suspended or confiscated and the editors imprisoned. The effects of this purge were seen in the reduced number of papers that began to publish after 1887 (when the Componte ended).

The years 1888-1898 were years of crisis for Puerto Rican journaliam because it was during that time that the press tried to re-orient itself after the Componte. Twenty papers were founded but they were poor and short-lived. Figuratively, the editors were groping in the dark, searching for a line of action which would gain subscribers and at the same time keep the paper in the good graces of the authorities. By 1890, the re-organization was complete and the Puerto Rican press had embarked upon a course of action completely different from that prior to 1887. There was one attempt made, however, to return to the journalism of the style before the Componte. This was La Razón, 1890-1891, of Mayagüez which was the last doctrinaire paper of the old school.

Its editor was Mario Braschi who was an excellent newspaperman, debater, reformer, and liberal. He was a man of firm ideals who never refused to enter into a journalistic combat; his place was in the vanguard at all times. He always maintained the principles of honor and patriotism

---

* 'Grito' is a term in Latin-America meaning a call to arms. The "Grito de Lares" was a call to arms in Lares, P.R. with the purpose of establishing a provisional government of republican character, September 23, 1868.

and belonged to that type of newspaperman who places honor before profit and honesty before sensationalism. He was the last crusader of the rationalistic and doctrinaire type of journalism. His type of paper was replaced in 1890 by the commercial newspaper in which abstract political articles were the exception and news was the rule. In 1890 news and advertising came into their own; the reporter first appeared, encroaching upon the prominence of the "redactor"; cable dispatches began to occupy more space; involved editorials on obscure points disappeared; and an appeal was made to the people as a whole and not to the few. In other words news triumphed over ideas, the Age of Reason was past and the Age of Headlines was at hand.

It would seem that the Puerto Rican press followed the dictates of progress far in advance of the government. The press transformed itself from a rather bombastic type of journalism into one of a literary and critical type. The editors seized upon all questions and problems and discussed them in so far as the censors would allow. The academic tone of the pre-1888 editorials was replaced by one which was sharp and witty because such was the demand of the new era. The editorial met a great rival in the news of the day. The public after 1890 demanded something more than dogmatic ideas from its journalism. Editorials had to stand the test of criticism of a more exacting public. Along with the editorial policy, principles, and standards the paper had to offer the public the news about the latest events. Weekly and tri-weekly papers had to change into dailies in order to satisfy the new demands. Informative replaced combative journalism. The press had to prove that it was the echo of public opinion and not of a particular editor with an ax to grind. Information about daily events came to occupy the preferential places which had been occupied with the absolute autocracy by ideas and doctrines. Political, economic, and social life (previously ignored) now began to demand publicity.

As a part of this new and energetic journalism there appeared a different kind of newspaper name. The following newspapers were founded during the period 1890-1898 and illustrate the different slant of insular journalism: Las Noticias, El Telegrama, El Noticiero, La Publicidad, La Información, El Cablegrama, and La Última Hora. No longer did names like El Clamor del País, El Agente, La Integridad Nacional, or La Crónica suffice. Although headlines never penetrated into Puerto Rican journalism until the coming of the Americans, 1890 saw the introduction of a more enticing title for articles. "Nuestra Café" or "Los Estados Unidos" no longer inspired the readers' interest. New titles which were in marked contrast with the old were as follows: "La Inquisición en los Estados Unidos", "99 Latigazos", "¡Que se extirpe!", "¡Locura!", and "El último cartucho".

Other changes manifested themselves after 1890. In so far as the layout of the paper was concerned, that year witnessed the increase of permanent sections. Editors no longer gave full reign to their imagination when sources were at stake but now used such terms as 'it is said', 'it is rumored', or 'according to our informants'. Advertising began to be increasingly important in the Puerto Rican paper during this period.

As has been mentioned, new items replaced the old doctrinaire editorials. Papers now were interested in the new and frequent political assemblies in the island, in the division of the parties, in the celebration of the centenaries of the discovery of America and Puerto Rico, and in the numerous duels. Editors fought monopolies and encouraged the foundation of co-operatives. Frequent strikes of newspaper workers occurred;

the workers' movement had its first beginning; and political points of view and debates multiplied. The papers of the new era were expected to report all in detail. As might be expected, that wave of public curiosity widened the geographic interests of Puerto Rico. The foreign correspondent was a logical result of this new journalism whose readers awaited anxiously the news of the Junta Revolucionaria of New York, of the Cuban War, of the diplomatic relations between Spain and the United States, and international politics in general.

The great number of papers reduced the number of subscribers, who could now pick and choose. Customers were sought in the street, homes, and places of business. The old journalism depended primarily on subscribers for existence; the new depended on advertisements and street sales, a condition which still persists in Puerto Rican newspapers. The vast number of publications had an ill effect upon the finance department of the paper; the great task of the new era was to get the subscriber to pay. The problems of the press were further complicated by the amount of illiteracy in the island. In 1860, 8.8% of the people were literate; in 1887, 13.8% and in 1899, 16.6%. These statistics are applied to a population which in 1899 was estimated to be 953,243. The lack of good roads, the censorship, the high cost of paper, and the infinite number of stamp-taxes in addition to the high illiteracy figures constantly threatened to drive the Puerto Rican editor to despair.[2]

Several papers and men figure prominently in the transformation of the Puerto Rican press after 1890. La Democracia, edited by Luis Muñoz Rivera, crusaded against monopolies, the electoral law, the lottery, the abuses and injustices of the mayors, and Spanish autocracy in general. Such a policy brought not only prestige and subscribers for the paper but also duels, denouncements, fines, and imprisonment for its editors. The fines, many times, were paid by popular subscription. Muñoz Rivera, a conviced Autonomist, believed in the formation of a pact or alliance with a Spanish liberal party which, he thought, would quicken autonomy for Puerto Rico. From 1896 to 1898 the policy of the paper was dedicated to bringing about such a pact. It finally came in the Sagasta Pact which split the Autonomist party in Puerto Rico into two groups--those who sided with Muñoz Rivera and those who remained faithful to the ideal of complete autonomy as proclaimed by the party. The probable benefits of the Pact speedily disappeared with the Spanish-American War.

El País was founded in 1895 by a group of men who opposed Muñoz Rivera's plans for autonomy. They felt that the best way to achieve autonomy was through the efforts of an autonomist party that would be completely independent from Peninsular politics. Puerto Rico, they maintained, should solve its problems from the Puerto Rican point of view and not from that of any Spanish party. It was their contention that the policies of parties in the Peninsula and in Puerto Rico were very different, that the island could best be served by independent action, and that in case of union Puerto Rico would receive but minor scraps from the Peninsular politicians.

Francisco Cepeda, the founder of La Revista de Puerto Rico, was another newspaperman who had a great effect on insular journalism. His interest, like that of Ramón B. López of La Correspondencia de Puerto Rico, was to make money in the newspaper business and not to argue political polemics. If circulation was decreasing, the paper immediately published a sensational article that landed the editor in jail. The rest of the papers of the island then called him a patriot and a martyr, the public paid his fine, subscriptions multiplied, advertisements were paid in advance, and the editor returned to his office well compensated for his days in jail. Naturally this policy had to be pursued with the greatest circumspection, but Cepeda was a master of that art.

On the other hand, papers like El Clamor del País with serious articles written by the best writers of Puerto Rico, languished and were on the point of bankruptcy innumerable times. There was more of the martyr than of the journalist in those papers but Cepeda's La Revista de Puerto Rico continued in its dual role of both martyr and newspaper.

La Correspondencia de Puerto Rico was founded in 1890 and quickly made a place for itself in Puerto Rican journalism. In fact, it brought about a minor revolution within the ranks of the insular press. It is the oldest daily in existence in Puerto Rico, although it does not enjoy the distinction of being the oldest daily paper of the island. Until the foundation of La Correspondencia de Puerto Rico the papers of Puerto Rico were all party organs, engaged in a fierce political fight, usually publishing three times weekly. Each copy cost three cents. Naturally, these papers with their high price could not and did not reach the hands of all classes of the people. Then appeared La Correspondencia with its revolutionary change. The paper sold for one cent! It soon acquired a great circulation, since without occupying itself ostensibly with politics, it devoted itself chiefly to interesting news, recounted in a popular style. The rest of the papers saw in La Correspondencia a dangerous competitor because it was cheap and so widely read. Everyone read it. The rich and poor, the city and farm workers, the intellectuals and the businessmen all bought the paper, to the chagrin of the competing papers. The political periodicals all attacked the newcomer by calling it industrial in character and politically immoral. If, however, their explanation of 'industrial' and 'immoral' had anything to do with a wide circulation, the paper certainly deserved their criticism. In spite of their censure, the rest of the Puerto Rican press soon followed the example of La Correspondencia and transformed themselves into dailies and lowered their prices.

La Correspondencia followed a clever, non-committal policy. One day it published news that irritated the 'incondicionales'; the following day it had news which disgusted the Autonomists and pacified the reactionaries. Its editor, Ramón B. López, who did so much to transform Puerto Rican journalism was not a literary figure, a newspaperman, or a politician. He was a businessman whose object was to make money and not to debate the finer points of politics of literature. Although he was not a man of letters he had the gift of expressing himself so that the simplest reader could grasp a situation with the minimum amount of reading. In that way one might say that he was the first of the modern editors of ear--a sort of Puerto Rican Pulitzer. The men of the paper professed advanced political views but the main interest of the paper was news--and circulation. Everything was subordinated to news that would interest the public, to the informing of the public of what went on in the island and in the world.

In Puerto Rico editors had much to contend with for the cause of journalistic truth. Before the days of the press services in Puerto Rico press relations were slow and halting to say the least. Cable rates were high and this method of communication was discouraged by censorship. As a result it was customary to print news letters from correspondents in New York and other American cities. The life of the Puerto Rican editors was rendered far from pleasant because of daily struggles with governmental censorship, capricious officials, the vast number of would be editors of 'fly-by-night' papers, and a public which, due to the superfluity of newspapers, usually subscribed but did not pay.

A leading Autonomist and one of the leaders in Puerto Rican journalism, commented sarcastically upon newspaper conditions in Puerto Rico. He felt that in the island, where the institutions were preserved from the times of Ponce de Leon, only the aristocracy and bureaucracy ate well while the newspapermen and teachers ate not at all. Braschi's articles had the pungent, biting character of a crusading editor who fought well and had a clear insight into the troubles of the day but who, like most crusaders, died poor. His contemporaries felt that any writer with half the brains which he squandered in his daily struggle with the conservative Puerto Rican press could have made a fortune for himself and his family in any other country in the world---especially the United States.

Braschi elaborated upon editorial troubles. He reproduced an article from the <u>New York World</u> to the effect that "one third of the people believe that they can handle a criminal case better than a lawyer; one half believe that they can cure a sick person better than a doctor; two-thirds believe that they can govern the republic better than the president, and all of them believe that they can direct a paper better than its editor." He went on to say that the same thing applied to Puerto Rico and that the <u>New York World</u> had certainly told the truth. Finally, the editor figuratively threw up his hands in the following article:

"If I defend autonomy, they don't like it. If I talk about the McKinley Bill, the people are tired of reading about it. If I say that the Catholic Congress stinks, the priests and old ladies who live in the church all the time attack me. Meanwhile, the subscribers are yelling to high heaven because of the poor quality of the column. So I cannot be with my thumbs crossed like the Chamber of Commerce with the Yankee question because I would be kicked out of the paper. Now, I ask you, God, with what can I fill this column?"[2]

Certain years stand out prominently in the crowded era of 1890 to 1898. In 1890 the government reduced the tax on cablegrams for papers, thus greatly facilitating the diffusion of news. 1895 was a year of unjust and celebrated trials; two of the most flagrant examples of the injustices of that year were those of Mariano Abril and Izcoa Díaz. 1897 was the beginning of the workers' press, directed by workers and devoted exclusively to labor propaganda and to social justice. There were many labor papers before 1897 but they had isolated purposes and none of them defended the emancipation of the worker from organized capital. There was no 'party line', then, before 1897. The founder of the new labor movement was Santiago Iglesias Pantín. 1898 was decisive for the history of Puerto Rico and for Puerto Rican journalism. The Autonomist government was inaugurated in February by virtue of the Sagasta Pact which was productive of a break in the Autonomist Party and of such a violent press struggle between the parties that Governor-General Macías had to intervene.

The political leaders knew what they wanted by 1898, which helps to account for the violence of the party quarrels of that year. The liberals had attained their autonomy with the granting of political decentralization through the autonomy chart of 1897. Unfortunately the international situation was to change the whole course of affairs and the island found itself suddenly involved in an international struggle in which it had no part. The provisional government which was to inaugurate autonomy in Puerto Rico was established February 11, 1898, four days before the "Maine", the event which practically began the Spanish-American War.

Elections were held on March 25, 1898, one month before McKinley sent his declaration of war to Congress; the new government met to legisl-late for the island one week before the American troops landed on the southern end of the island, July 25, 1898. The American army was feted from there to the capital, San Juan, and in December of 1898 the island was ceded to the United States in the Treaty of Paris. The autonomy experiment came to an end and Puerto Rico was to start on a new period of colonial experimentation.

(1) Pedreira, Antonio S.: El Periodismo en Puerto Rico, 135 ff.
(2) Pedreira, Antonio S.: El Periodismo en Puerto Rico, p. 143.

The Yankee Press

There was quite a division of opinion among the Puerto Rican publicists regarding the United States' press. This division followed roughly the cleavage between the conservatives and the liberals. The conservatives criticized and found fault most of the time; the liberals admired the American press with its freedom, liberalism, and tendency to print all the news available but criticized, at the same time, the American tendency to print much that they considered unfit to publish. This last was deplored but in general excused by the good points already mentioned.

There was the feeling that the newspaper press of the world had reached its highest development in the United States. It was felt that, if one were to judge by the number of publications and subscribers in the United States, enterprises of that sort progressed the most in North America. By way of proof figures were cited to prove this point; of some 4,964 papers in the world, 1,759 of them were in the United States alone.[1]

On the one hand the liberals saw in the United States a freedom of the press, a prosperous life for most editors, and palatial newspaper buildings; on the other they saw in Puerto Rico censorship, newspaper poverty, and their own temporary print-shops. It is easy to understand the Puerto Rican journalists' feeling of envy and longing for a system whereby editorials would not have to run the risk of suppression and the editors the risk of jail.[2] That is one reason for the detailed description given to the office of the New York Herald and also for the account of the rise to fame and fortune of Joseph Pulitzer and his New York World.

Joseph Pulitzer was felt to be something of a giant in the newspaper world and his paper, the New York World, received very favorable comment in the Puerto Rican press. The fact that one man could take over a paper and make a mighty institution of it in ten years was a miracle. Even the advertisements in his paper were felt to be full of interest. The size of the staff, the many reporters, the newsgathering service, and the modern and efficient methods of operation were things that the Puerta Rican papers mentioned constantly as marvels. The World's treatment of political topics seemed to reflect the political life of the world and there seemed to be no reform which it did not favor. Although the conservative press of Puerto Rico bitterly condemned Pulitzer's paper, they grudgingly admitted that it had a great influence in the world.

The progressiveness of American papers was frankly admitted by Manuel Fernández Juncos of El Buscapié when he said that he was publishing some articles from the United States together with some prints from American engravers so that they might work as an encouraging factor for the Puerto Rican press.[3] This spirit of 'go ahead' as illustrated by American papers was generally recongnized and imitated by the liberal editors.[4]

On every possible occasion the conservative Boletín ridiculed the idea of a free press which the Autonomist catechism emphasized. The Boletín's position as a semi-official organ of the government exempted it from any of the censorship regulations. At any rate, it followed the practice of agreeing with the Spanish authorities at all times so that the censors inspired little fear. Freedom of the press, then, was anathema to this paper and it lost no opportunity to point out the evils of such a thing in articles entitled "La prensa en los países libre. " The free countries referred to were the South American republics, which were more free and republican in theory than in practice. Therefore, it reasoned, freedom of the press, meant license and guidance only by the dictations of caprice, as was alleged to be the case in South America. What good, then, did it do to have such beautiful but unworkable theories? [5]

The following article illustrates, in general, what many Puerto Ricans thought about the American reading habit, about the operation of the Yankee press, and about the American as compared with European papers.

"Reading to the American people is more than a custom, it is a necessity. A true Yankee is he who has his pockets full of newspapers, pamphlets, and books. In the street-car, in the railroad coach, in between the intermission of the shows, in the quiet of his home, every place where the North American is one may find him with a book or a paper. That is the reason for the great importance acquired by publications in that country. That is why newspapers there make so much money. Those who have travelled know the value of the New York Herald and the New York World. Nothing of doctrinaire articles, nor of philosophy, or of useless polemics is found in those papers. The Yankee wants to know in the least amount of time what is going on in the world. He will think himself very unhappy when he retires if he does not know how the Khedive of Egypt or the Emperor of Germany felt and how many degrees the thermometer had gone down in Moscow, and what horse won in London, and what la Patti sang in the opera, or how much flour sold for in Santander.... [6]

In addition to the fact that liberal Puerto Ricans found much to admire in American journalism, most of the Puerto Rican editors looked with envy on American journalists because of the high salaries paid to American editors, assistant editors, and reporters. American papers were reputed to pay their editors at least fifteen thousand dollars per year, the assistant editors a little less, and even the reporters five thousand, according to the Puerto Rican reports. The idea that newspapermen earned more than did teachers, that there were more employees on the staff of the New York World than there were in the Department of Interior of Puerto Rico was quite incomprehensible.[7]

The fact that American journalism has always had a character all its own was recognized by the Puerto Rican press. The American practice of sending special ambassadors to interview heads of states was something of a shock to newspapermen who were impressed with official formality. [8]

Salvador Brau, the editor of El Clamor del País, realized the profound difference between the press of the United States and of Puerto Rico. Consistent attacks on anyone or any nation was not the way of American journalism. On the contrary, the American public demanded something new and different each day. Their news had to be clear. concise, and to the point. A headline was an absolute necessity. Puerto Rican journalism could carry on a consistent campaign upon almost any topic, such as the McKinley Bill, loyalty to Spain, or the necessity of making Puerto Rican coffee known in the United States. Those topics needed no headline. People subscribed to the paper because of their political beliefs or friendship with the editor but very rarely because one paper had better news than another paper.

The sensationalism of the American jingo press was regarded with many misgivings by all the papers in Puerto Rico. As a result, Puerto Rican antagonism to American journalism was due mostly to the sensationalism of the yellow press of the era. When insignificant events were inflated into hair-raising stories, it is small wonder that the foreigner received a poor impression of the American way of life.

A bungled execution by means of the electric chair at Sing Sing appeared as a sensational story in American papers. In Puerto Rican papers it was received with mixed feelings, but it was certainly no sensational story. It was hailed as an example of barbarism by the conservatives; the liberals deplored this use of science.[9] A Puerto Rican news account of a particularly gory murder was considered an example of the pernicious Yankee influence upon insular journalism.[10] The Puerto Rican reader expected to find a special list of daily executions if he read an American paper.[11] This was due largely to stories about the Wild West, lynchings, labor riots as at Homestead, and Indian massacres. Peace and quiet was something that did not exist in the United States.

However, a vague feeling of apprehension pervaded the Puerto Rican press in regard to Yankee papers. This apprehension was caused by many and varied incidents. Events ranging from novel circulation promotion projects and the typical covering of executions to the downright agitation for the United States' declaration of war by the yellow press caused uneasiness among conservatives and liberals alike.

Americans are used to unusual schemes adopted by newspapers to increase their circulation, but foreigners have never quite become accustomed to such procedures, especially if the gentler sex is envolved. The New York World decided to imitate Jules Verne and his trip around the world by sending a reporter, Nellie Bly, on the same trip. This was thought to be an unusual 'stunt', but at the same time it was admitted of having possibilities, as it was recalled that Pulitzer had taken over an almost bankrupt paper and had made it into a figure of importance by just such ideas. Of course, his business ability was given recognition.

The offering of rewards for the best recipe to keep husbands at home was another project which aroused comment, to the extent that El Clamor del País broke away from its Latin conservatism to offer a recipe of its own. It advised the wife to beg the husband to go out all the time---then he would stay home.[12]

The incident between the United States and Italy over the lynching of some Italian sailors in New Orleans was offered as an example of the extent to which the yellow press would go to make news. The sensible press of the United States condemned the actions at New Orleans and urged that the guilty be punished. At that point the liberal press in Puerto Rico took the opportunity to indulge in a little homily on government in general, comparing law enforcement in autocratic and liberal countries. The fact that the conscientious press in the United States condemned the murders and urged Secretary of State Blaine to do something about that blot on the name of New Orleans was indicative of a strong public morality. This, it said, is impossible in countries where the courts of justic can not function free from political pressure and bribery. It is not with rifles and bayonets that the inviolability of the law is imposed, continued the liberals, but by obedience and respect. The barometer of the morality of a people must be found in the antecedents of a government because where lies, abuses, and frauds are the order of the day, government will be nothing more than racketeering. But, it concluded, "like everything in this immense country, this deed has passed away from the stage and the press now is full of topics which make people forget that blot on the record of the model republic...." [13] Thus was indicated the transient character of the news in American life.

The representation by the American jingo press that the filibusters for a free Cuba were somehow brothers under the skin of the patriots who fought under Washington at Valley Forge did not find very fertile ground either in Mexico or in Puerto Rico. One filibuster was not much different from any other in the eyes of the Latin-Americans. [14]

Every small-time Cuban revolutionary was given more importance than he deserved in the American news, much to the disgust of the Spanish authorities. Filibustering expeditions were given the halo of crusades and the Cuban patriots in New York, Key West, and Tampa were lionized as heroes. [15] Just what was the Puerto Rican press to believe about either the United States or the American press?

Sensible literary papers felt that the Americans and their press were gullible to believe the reports as given out by the adventurers with everything to gain and nothing to lose. [16] It was small wonder, then, that most Puerto Rican readers should be suspicious of such news, and that at any event news emanating from those sources should not be trusted. [17]

Conservatives like the Boletín Mercantil lost no opportunity to criticize the Yankees. An example of this was a reference made by an American paper to the fact that the 'first press' was established at Cambridge, Massachusetts, in 1639. This statement, the Boletín declared to be false, misleading, and presumptuous, as anyone should have known that it was the Spaniards who established the 'first press' in the New World in Mexico in 1535. It was felt that the Yankees, by printing such a statement, were trying to steal some of the glory that rightfully belonged to Spain. [18]

Criticism of the United States was always abundant in the Conservative press, even at the time of the Columbian Exposition, when relations between the two countries were supposedly at their best. The conservatives rather justified themselves at the time by saying that even the mother Anglo-Saxon nation, Great Britain, criticized the United States, a fact which somehow removed any Exposition-imposed restrictions on that score. [19]

Conservatives felt that the American press had never heard of the law of libel or at least of unwritten rules of international press courtesy. The fact that American imagination was stirred by stories of 'heroic' bands of Cuban rebels fighting in the swamps against the Guardia Civil and that these stories might be interpreted as the Cuban counterpart of the history of the Great American West never occurred to conservative editors. They always resented those accounts as calumniations from afar by persons whose only intent was to overthrow the Spanish regime in the Antilles by writing in such safe places as New York, Philadelphia, and Key West. These reports were regarded as slanders upon decent persons by men of no culture. [20]

The liberals, on the other hand, eagerly awaited news from the States. They wanted to know what was happening between the United States and Spain and believed that their government purposely took advantage of Puerto Rico's insular position to keep them in ignorance. "We are interested in knowing what the Yankee press thinks about us" was a much repeated comment among the liberals. [21] Such New York papers as the <u>New York Times</u>, the <u>New York World</u>, the <u>Herald</u>, and the <u>Sun</u> were quoted time after time. Whenever a Puerto Rican liberal desired to express his views and run little risk of being thrown into jail by an exasperated Spanish government he would quote an American paper. Thus censorship was eluded and the liberal conscience was saved by the device of making the American paper alone responsible. This does not mean that those quotations actually appeared in the American paper. The cited papers were merely the front for a public opinion that was determined to express itself.

Public opinion in the United States was something that was admired by the liberal press and viewed with alarm by the conservative. At the same time, a public opinion that could influence the government was regarded as something of a wonder. The Latin concept of authority has always been different from the Anglo-Saxon. Therefore, it was difficult to understand how the newspapers could sway a government that had been placed in power by the people or how these elected representatives of the nation could permit newspaper attacks. Some Puerto Rican papers had a naive opinion of the influence of official visits and dinners. The visit of the Spanish Infantas to the United States in 1893 was expected to have far reaching consequences upon Spanish-American relations. [22] The attitude of European nations toward American intervention in Cuba was expected to act as a restraining influence upon the American public. [23]

Some papers came out with a flat warning not to trust American public opinion as expressed in the newspapers because, they said, a great part of that press favors the independence of Cuba as does a majority of the Yankee people. But, it continued, that majority does not include the big-businessmen who disapprove of the ideas of the politicians as being harmful to commerce. For industrial kings it would be more convenient from a business standpoint to see Cuba remain Spanish than for it to become independent. Most of the time, those papers went on, the industrialists controlled governmental policy. The real danger was that the government might be forced to act, due to a sudden outburst of what it termed radical public opinion. [24]

General relations between the Puerto Rican and the American press depended on various factors. Puerto Rican interest in the United States fluctuated. Such incidents as the McKinley Bill, the Venezuelan trouble between England and the United States, the Chicago Fair of 1893, and the Cuban Revolt of 1895 were periods of intense interest in the attitude of the Northern Republic. The sinking of the "Maine", naturally, falls into this category.

The period of normal interest included both the prosaic and spectacular. Indian fighting, cattle-rustling, and western life in general have always impressed the foreigner, no matter what he thought of American government and politics. Stories of violent and sudden death in the Great Republic were always good copy for foreign papers. There was also a desire to know something about a country whose vast size and material progress produced a vague fear of what then, as now, is termed the 'Colossus of the North'. Of course the extent of this fear was conditioned by the political faith of the foreign reader.

There were times when all papers in the United States and Puerto Rico were in agreement, although those times were few and far between.

The first instance of this in reference is shown when the Infantas of Spain visited the Columbian Exposition. Visiting nobility has always exerted a powerful attraction over the imagination of the American democracy, and this visit was no exception. Most of the American papers, as a matter of course, made much over this visit. It was good copy, a boost for the Fair, and did not involve any controversial question. In addition, journalists realized the natural weakness of their readers for something new and different, that is, the visit of the Spanish princesses to the United States and made capital out of it. The Puerto Rican papers, naturally, were flattered by the attention paid to the Infantas and to other noble visitors by the "industrial and mercantile republic of Washington".[25]

Spanish Moroccan policy afforded another example of agreement. The New York Herald supported Spain in that affair. The Boletín Mercantil made several about faces there, apparently without realizing it. They complimented the Herald on its stand for several reasons: first, because it was a colossus in the American newspaper world and everything that it said was important and true; second, it did justice to Spain because it outlined a course of action for Spain in Morocco which was in accordance with the national dignity and honor (and, incidentally, gave Spain her rightful place in the African sun); third, it justified Spanish intervention in Morocco because of the many insults the Moors had given the Spanish government.[26]

Later, with the beginning of the Cuban Revolt in 1895, the Herald was not so high in the graces of the conservative papers; apparently the American place in the sun of the Caribbean had no relation with the Spanish place in the sun of Morocco. Every American paper of importance (and many of lesser influence) was quoted on the Cuban question.

Any paper which thought that it was a crazy desire of the United States to buy Cuba, that all political parties in Spain would unite whenever Cuba was in danger, and that Spain would spend her last peseta and send her last soldier to death rather than lose the Pearl of the Antilles was quoted in full and shown to be a true intellectual of intellectuals.[27]

Las Novedades, a conservative Spanish paper in New York City, always gave full accounts of the capture of any Cuban rebel,[28] the brave exploits of the Guardia Civil, or a speech from the throne. If any of these appeared in the New York Times in a favorable light it was sure to be highly approved by papers like the Boletín in Puerto Rico.[29] At such times, Pan-Americanism was always at its highest.

Autonomy was always a controversial question. In general, the American papers favored some kind of an agreement between Spain and Cuba which would give Cuba a measure of self-government while the Puerto Rican conservatives, on the other hand, could reply that Cuba was quiet.[30] Paraphrasing Cromwell's statement, Cuba was pacified---or quiet until 1895.

Some American papers, such as the New York Tribune, declared that the United States was a saturated state and needed no more annexations or conquests of a territorial nature. This, it felt, was especially true of conquests any place south of the border, since any annexations would only incorporate erratic and turbulent peoples into the calm and practical Anglo-Saxon nation. In response, most Spanish papers accused the Tribune of merely promoting an underhanded policy of concealing the real aim of political union with bombastic phrases. [31]

The New York Sun persisted "in its chimerical, foolish, and ambitious dream for the annexation of Cuba by the Yankee colossus".[32] For some reason this paper seemed to have a strong aversion towards all that was Spanish, except its desire for Cuba. It published arguments pro and con concerning various islands that the United States might need as naval bases. The Bermudas, Jamaica, Haiti. Santo Domingo were all considered, but each was ruled out for one reason or another and Cuba alone was favored. Such arguments in American journals convinced the Puerto Ricans of the nefarious intentions of the North American republic upon one of the remnants of Spain's once great empire in the New World.[33] As though this were not enough to strain relations between the two nations, Cuban revolutionary propaganda always was given space in the American papers. This caused much uneasiness and wrath in Spain. [34]

American papers and the American people were accused of tilting with wind-mills and of pursuing will-o'-the wisps over the world in search of such Holy Grails as democracy, Cuban independence, our way of life etc., etc., ad infinitum. It was incomprehensible that such a mercantile, industrial, and pre-eminently practical nation as the United States would lend itself to such projects. Spanish papers, it was felt, absorbed some of this quality because they showed a wishful thinking attitude in regard to the quality and strength of the Yankee fleet whenever that fleet was compared with the Spanish. What they said about the Yankee fleet was one thing and what happened was another. The Spanish papers proved, to their own satisfaction, that when and if the Spanish ships abuilding were built, Spain would be the greatest naval power in the world, far ahead of the United States and England. [35]

News coming from the United States' papers was felt to be one-sided in regard to the Cuban revolution. That news which portrayed, for the most part, Spanish reverses during the rebellion, was conducive to the lowering of the prestige of the Spanish army in Cuba and Puerto Rico and advantageous to the rebels. [36] This "furious news spirit" of the American press, [37] the interviews of the leaders of Cuban 'laborantismo' in the United States,[38] and the yellow journalism then in vogue in the North were causes of bitter complaints both in Cuba and in Puerto Rico. The attitude of the people and the papers of the United States was felt to be the same--- friendship for the rebels and a feeling that the only way to settle the Cuban problem was for Spain to grant Cuba its independence. Naturally this was answered by articles showing that the Yankee papers were exaggerating the importance of the revolt and that the rebels were not men of intelligence but were demagogues who could not hope to win.[39]

Liberal papers in Puerto Rico lamented their dearth of information concerning Cuba and complained that their only sources of information were the official Spanish dispatches and the reports of American papers. The obvious and prompt reply of the conservatives was that the liberals should take all American versions of the revolt with a pound of salt as those reports were invented stories and undependable.[40] To prove their contention, interviews of American tourists were published. These interviews were intended to show that the revolt in Cuba existed mostly in the minds of North American journalists and that it was of no more importance than a riot of dock workers in New York.

American papers followed the practice of interviewing leading men in regard to the Cuban situation. General Martínez Campos was interviewed and his views were commented upon and given much space in the New York papers. General Martínez Campos' views were as follows:

"Promises which are never fulfilled, abuses of all kinds, the neglect of progress, the exclusion of the natives from the administration, and many other mistakes gave origin to the Cuban revolt. The belief of the government has continued that there was no other means than terror and that dignity prevented the introduction of any reforms as long as there was fighting. In that way we can never conclude the war even if the island were inhabited by soldiers. I believe that if Cuba is too small to be independent it can be at least a Spanish province.... [41]

Peninsular papers lamented about the inexact news that was published in the United States, which only excited the people and did much to provoke a war with Spain.[42] The theory of the American papers that the free should help the unfree was not understood. That policy of helping the under-dog was inexplicable when compared with the status of the negroes, Indians, and Chinese in the United States. The only explanation they could offer was that American enthusiasm for the Cubans was of a commercial and materialistic nature---that humanitarianism was not a factor. It was explained that the American tobacco growers in Cuba desired either the independence or the annexation of Cuba to the United States in order to restore their prosperity. Even the liberal Puerto Rican papers talked against the American encouragement and assistance of the rebellion. They felt that the best way to attain liberty and prosperity was to follow the methods of law and peace, not those of riot and bloodshed. [43]

It was the general opinion that, if one read only the comments of the American press about the war, a bad opinion concerning Spaniards would be formed; that the actions of Congressmen and politicians who felt that Spain was forcing a war with the United States were based on misinformation. However, according to El Liberal, those men were fanatics: the thinking people believed that the United States was not prepared for war and did not want one. [44]

American papers were accused of making a common practice of sending out false and sensational information. The Puerto Rican conservative press pointed out the danger that such practices might lose all public credence in such journals. But they felt that even this danger meant little to the North American press since the American public was extremely credulous. Therefore any attempt to save the New York papers from themselves was just so much wasted effort. Rumors were in circulation that Spain might voluntarily renounce her sovereignty over Cuba because she realized that her position was hopeless. These rumors were always attributed to the New York papers.

All sorts of rumors were circulated by the New York Herald, one that Spain had decided to claim an indemnity from the United States and England for permitting fillibustering expeditions to sail from their shores. This was ridiculed by the Puerto Rican papers who said that Spain would never be one to provoke a war by making unreasonable claims but that Spain was only interested in the defense of her legitimate rights in the Antilles and in nothing more. [45] Another was that the United States would no longer tolerate the unjust and discriminating treatment accorded its citizens in Cuba but would demand a great indemnity. These reputed demands were played up by the jingo press to such an extent that many people in the United States and in Puerto Rico could not distinguish between official intentions and newspaper hysteria.

Those rumored demands for indemnities immediately started reporters in Puerto Rico to work figuring up the total number of filibustering expeditions that had sailed from American ports during that particular year. The logical result would be, naturally, that the one to demand an indemnity was not the United States but Spain.[46]

The friendship of the American press for the Cubans and their struggle for independence was repeatedly decried by papers like the Boletín Mercantil, La Balanza, and La Integridad Nacional. The attitude of these papers was that the Cubans were bandits committing arson and murder and deserving of nothing but court martial.[47]

Many Cubans took refuge in American citizenship in order to carry on their separatist agitation both in Cuba and in the United States. This led to constant troubles between the Spanish authorities and American consul in Habana. The Spaniards felt that the separatists should be judged by a court martial in spite of the fact that they were American citizens, while the American consul took the stand that they should be tried by a civil court. A common complaint in this connection was that the representations that were made by the consul were made in an incorrect form and one which lacked friendship. As a result several of the consuls were 'persona non grata' to the Spanish government, and their recall was requested. Immediately the American press suggested that a better procedure would be to send several battleships to Habana to make General Calleja and the Cuban government reasonable. Suggestions of this sort were sure to raise the editorial blood pressure in Puerto Rico and to be productive of declarations of Spanish glory, dignity, and honor.[48]

It was felt that the jingo papers had only one purpose. This was to influence the government to recognize the belligerency of the Cuban rebels and thus to provoke Spain to war.[49] The Herald tried to form a favorable public opinion towards the Cuban exiles and advocated the formation of an anti-Spanish movement in the Latin-American republics---especially in Mexico. Mexico, El País pointed out, did not react very favorably to those overtures from the United States, because past experience had taught her that American emancipation usually took the form of annexation of territory. Anglo-Saxon crusades to save some one were more likely to result in treaties beneficial to only the United States. The Treaty of Guadalupe-Hidalgo was more present in Mexican thoughts than any anxiety over the status of Cuba or the possibility that Spain might seize Mexico and use it as a base of operations in a war against the United States.[50]

Ulterior motives were ascribed to the American press for favoring a free Cuba. It was thought that the press was venal and that Cuban bonds were given to papers as payment for inflamatory articles. Even Congressmen were reported to have accepted those bonds, and the Department of State was accused of knowing about the matter. The bonds were 'sold' to influential people, many of them paying a nominal sum, others accepting them as a gift. Altruism, according to one paper,[51] was not involved. The main idea was profit with no humanitarian or noble motives. Such an affair seemed credible in view of the operations of the Crédit Mobilier which implicated many prominent persons in its national swindle. Good and bad people alike participated in that organized pillage of the Federal Treasury, and it was conceivable that the same thing was being repeated on a smaller scale with the Cuban bonds.[52]

Hostility on the part of the New York papers which never missed an opportunity to be hostile to Spain was felt acutely in Puerto Rico. An often repeated point was that the United States ought to occupy Habana if Spain did not pay the Mora claim, a claim which most papers in Puerto Rico thought unjust.[53] Puerto Ricans thought that Spanish power and glory of the past was something that the United States should envy. Some papers believed, however, that this envy was being compensated in many ways, such as by American prosperity, material achievements, and the clear intention of the United States to see that Spain did not eclipse American moral influence in the New World.[54]

American criticism of the Spanish government in the Antilles immediately touched off angry protests from the conservatives. Thus Puerto Rican papers devoted a great deal of space to answering what was considered attacks on Spanish honor, dignity, and prestige. One such incident concerned an article published in a New York paper attacking the reputation and capabilities of the Customs' employees in Puerto Rico. The Puerto Rican answer was to the effect that the New York paper should secure better information when the reputation of a noble people was involved.[55]

Sometimes such answer over-reached itself and revealed the real rea- son for the controversy. Governmental anarchy, said a New York paper, existed in Puerto Rico because of the arbitrary application of the suffrage laws. This, replied the Boletín Mercantil, was unjust as well as false be- cause "this José Escobar, who was excluded from the voters' list and who was an official of the government, deserved nothing better. Besides, he was an Autonomist and, therefore, an enemy of the government that pays him".[56] Apparently Autonomists had no right to expect anything else from the gov- ernment in Puerto Rico.

One American paper criticized the operations of the European parlia- ments, including that of the Spanish regime in the Antilles. Those parlia- ments were ridiculed as being farcial and of very little value. It was incom- prehensible to Puerto Ricans how this ridicule could be made in view of the noisy sessions of the House of Representatives, the existence of 'gag-rules' in a supposedly democratic chamber, and such scenes as fist fights in both the Senate and the House. This had never happened in the Cortes, even in the most troubled days of Spanish said the Boletín. On the contrary, all orators were heard in courteous silence, conducive to the development of speakers like Castelar, rivals of Cato and Demosthenes. Could it be pos- sible that the carping American press had forgotten those facts? The Amer- icans should reform their own legislative assemblies before they talked about others.[57]

"Cuba for Sale" was an attack that appeared in the New York Herald relative to the project of farming out the collection of the Cuban customs to the highest bidder, foreign or domestic. Here was a case of a foreigner meddling in an affair that was purely Spanish. This article was resented by the Puerto Rican press,[58] in spite of the fact that that press also attacked the idea and that a similar procedure was followed in San Juan in its garbage disposal. Pablo Ubarri, later made the Count of Santurce, purchased the right to collect the garbage of the city from the perenially hard-up govern- ment. If the inhabitants of the city did not see fit to pay the charges im- posed by Ubarri for the garbage disposal, their garbage piled higher and higher and they were subject to fine by the government. Although the article, "Cuba for Sale", was resented by the Puerto Rican press, the danger of allowing the collection of the customs to fall into the hands of the North Americans was realized. That was the right road to follow if Spain wanted to lose Cuba.

The Puerto Rican press deplored the actions of the yellow press. Those actions were held to be lucrative to the newspapers concerned but a disturbing factor to international finance and diplomatic relations and deserved the unanimous reprobation of all lovers of peace. The Puerto Rican papers were talking about a Renaissance in the Antilles, which was to be based on material and moral peace and to be productive of a new era of prosperity and riches. Of course, the Cuban revolt was to be settled first. Encouragement for this attitude was found in the words of isolated Congressmen who warned the United States not to think that Spain was an old, decrepit, and impotent nation, incapable of winning a war. Those men warned that the American policy of pin-pricks would cause Spain to burst finally, and difficulties would be created for the United States. They asked whether the jingo papers could justify with mere sentimentalism a war which would cost so much blood and so much perturbation to business. These men seemed to be voices crying in the wilderness, Jeremiahs who prophesied mournful events, but they were considered as traitors by the jingoes. The Puerto Rican press, on the other hand, called them true prophets and men who had correctly estimated Spanish vigor, bravery, and history.[59]

The sinking of the "Maine" was the great opportunity for the American jingoes. It was hard for them to keep public enthusiasm at the fever pitch indefinitely over such topics as the concentration camps in Cuba, Weyler and his methods, and humanity in general. The "Maine" was a God-send. They were now in the position of the righteous who could say "I told you so". The torpedo theory, the submarine mine charge, and others were advanced by them. Assistant-Secretary of the Navy Theodore Roosevelt averred that it was the sinister and intentional work of the enemies of the United States, a contention which certain investigators supported. The Spaniards were reported to have cut all cables between the Antilles and the United States, American nationals were insulted on the streets of Habana and San Juan, vague rumors had circulated about blowing up the "Maine" before it happened, the National Guard would soon be mobilized, and Spaniards in Habana were going to proclaim a holiday in honor of the tragedy. All those and more were the stories circulated by the sensational press of the United States which, naturally, were refuted by the Puerto Rican press.[60]

At that time the "Vizcaya" was making a good-will cruise to New York in return for the visit of the "Maine" to Habana. Now American papers drew up maps showing how that cruiser could destroy New York City in a very few hours and inflict a damage of at least three hundred million dollars. The papers demanded that the "Vizcaya" be anchored under the guns of a fort in New York harbor or at any rate near to an American warship of equal or greater fire power.[61]

Puerto Rican papers wanted to know how it happened that the "Maine' was full of munitions and how American efficiency explained the carelessness of the crew of the "Maine". It was felt that the jingo papers were bringing this verdict against Spain: "Not guilty, but do not do it again".[62]

Credit was given to the Spanish papers in New York such as Las Novedades and Cuba for protecting Spanish honor and for answering these blasts of the jingoes. Those papers were thanked for repulsing energetically the sophism of the Congressional debates, the fantastic stories in the news, and the alarms which the New York papers created for the rebel cause in Cuba.[63]

Foreign painters with Latin connections were attacked by the American press during the last few months before the war whenever they tried to exhibit their paintings in the United States. It was felt in Puerto Rico that the American customs' laws were deliberately used against those famous men and that Yankee protectionism was used in a discriminatory manner. This seemed to prove that the jingo party never forgot any means to provoke a conflict between the United States and the Old World. It was pointed out that many Americans went to Europe and became ex-patriates just to escape the troubles and vexations that such a press created.[64] Various persons were quoted to prove that the tales of the American press were untrue. One of them was a reporter of the New York Evening Post who was regarded by the Puerto Rican paper as a very famous and respectable person, one who knew Cuba and Puerto Rico perfectly, was impartial, and was an internationalist who could report about the true situation in the Antilles. He said that Habana and the rest of Cuba were tranquil and that in certain provinces the revolt had almost ended. This report was accepted as indisputable proof that there was no necessity for American intervention.[65]

All through the papers in the last few months before the war there was the feeling that the attitude of the United States was in danger of being formed by the sensational press, that it was creating a situation favorable for war, and that McKinley and Woodford, the American minister .o Spain, were exceptions to the rule.[66] Rafael María de Labra,* representative from Puerto Rico to the Spanish Cortes, appreciated this situation fully. He took note of the jingo agitation in the United States as being a greater threat to peace than the attitude of the president was a preventative to war. It was his opinion that jingo rumors were especially dangerous to peace. The rumors circulated (that the American consul could not answer for the safety of North Americans in Cuba after the "Maine", that Washington was thinking of sending several cruisers to be at the disposal of Consul Lee, and that Spain felt no regrets concerning the "Maine") were certainly not conducive to coherent thinking. Labra felt that this was a deliberate campaign calculated to arouse European sympathy for the United States and to cause European neutrality in case of war. He admitted that after all this had happened it was hard to erase the lies of the jingo press and to restore a situation approaching normalcy.[67]

The chapter on the influence of the American press is not complete without some reference to advertising and its influence upon Puerto Rico. Americans seemed to have learned the trick of sensational advertising before other peoples. The idea of convincing the public of the absolute necessity of buying a certain brand of tobacco in order to get the best possible quality rather took foreigners aback. It was with surprise that they read the flamboyant description of the superior qualities of Dr. Williams' pills or of a particular brand of cement. The safe and sure policy of foreign advertising contrasted with that of American sensationalism and conscientious boasting. The testimonial type of advertisement was, on the whole, an

---

*Rafael Maria de Labra y Cadrana, 1841-1918, was a member to the Spanish Cortes, 1871, 1886, and 1896. He was a convinced Autonomist and liberal, favored closer cultural and political ties between Spain and the Antilles, worked for the development of democracy through education, and urged the abolition of slavery (Spain abolished it in 1873). He was a noted political thinker and author of many books in political science.

American development. Army captains, bankers, and dock-workers all testified that they had been miraculously cured by the use of some Yankee medicine.[68] It was said that the United States was the one place in the world where the merits of advertising were best recognized. The Americans did not wait for clients to come. On the contrary, they sought clients with their ads.

The amounts of money involved in this business were felt to be stupendous, as some firms spent almost six hundred thousand dollars yearly on that alone. This willingness to spend so much money on a project which might or might not yield returns set the Yankees off in a place by themselves. The drug firm of Scott and Browne was cited as an example of this.[69]

Even the conservative paper, the Boletín Mercantil, admitted that one of the specialties of the United States was its indefatigable tendency for publicity. From that country came the electrically lighted bill-boards, which the paper thought to be sometimes incoherent, but which covered the walls of small stores and every visible surface It was asked whether the amount of money spent in that manner were comparable to the results. It questioned the value of the large number of ads necessary to convince a person that he was doing himself a good turn by buying another bar of soap of another cigar. American exploitation of misfortune for the sake of advertising was perhaps the most severely criticized. Another point of criticism was the American tendency to desecrate nature for the promotion of some one's new hair tonic or some such product. This was seen at the Chicago Fair when the Pulitzer Building illuminated the clouds merely to draw attention to the paper. This seemed to be approaching the delirious in the search for publicity.[70]

The progress of American advertising was noted. It was shown that an early New York paper, the Independent Gazette of 1787, had only thirty-four advertisements. After that date advertising was shown to be a legitimate necessity for the commerce of the United States. It was something unusual to see that some firms employed persons whose only purpose was to prepare advertisements for the papers. By 1891, it was noted that lithograph companies had also risen which supplied engravings for ads.[71] However, there was a saving grace for such enterprises. It was admitted to be undoubtedly true that advertising reduced the cost of papers and as a consequence had helped to diffuse news and general culture among the poorer classes. At the same time, it continued, the Yankees did not expect money to drop from Heaven and did their best to make money out of any kind of business, no matter how unusual or peculiar it might be.[72]

Peculiarity was demonstrated by the circumstance that the Singer Sewing Machine Company took advantage of the presentation of 'Faust' in New York in order to advertise its product. It was reported that they induced Margarita to use a Singer Machine instead of an old-fashioned spinning wheel! This seemed to prove that the Yankees lost no opportunity to propagandize their products.[73]

Operations could have been avoided according to ads in the Puerto Rican papers, if Dr. White's pills for dys epsia had been used. This seems to be carrying advertising a little too far, but it should be remembered that it was an American company which was involved. Almost anything could be expected from the Yankees.[74]

Even marriage was exploited. Several actors had been acting out a a marriage in the play that they had been performing for several weeks.

One day they decided to have a real wedding. This was well advertised, and, as may have been expected, according to the acid comment of the <u>Boletín Mercantil</u>, customers flocked to witness this travesty on religion.[75]

The never-ending feuds that the liberal and the conservative papers carried on is well illustrated by <u>La Razón</u> of Mayaguez. This paper noted that a fortune-teller advertised in a New York paper. <u>La Razón</u> suggested that this notice should be brought to the attention of the <u>Boletín</u> so that it could say a few things against the Yankees, the Monroe Doctrine, the lynch law, the poor Indians etc.[76]

In general most of the products advertised in Puerto Rico were European. Those products differed greatly from the American products in their method of advertising. There were no testimonials, stories, or miraculous cures attached to the European ads. In the ten year period that the writer studied, most ads of European products remained the same year after year with little or no variation. France held first place in all lines whether it was perfume, patent medicine, or tonic. England appeared with several products but seemed to have nothing as a specialty. Sweden advertised matches. The United States had such products for sale as Florida Water, bay-rum, Pasta Mack, tropical balm, tooth-paste, flour, liquid cement, coal-oil, bicycles, Eagle pencils, and watches. All kinds of pills were offered the insular consumer by the American drug firms of Holloway, Lanman & Kemp, Bristol, and Scott & Browne. The man with the fish on his back (Scott's Emulsion) is probably a more familiar advertisement in Puerto Rico than it is in the United States. It still occupies a 'must' position on the Puerto Rican medicine shelf. Bristol's Almanac (printed in Spanish) is a magazine which is regarded as infallible by the country people of Puerto Rico today. Its beginnings go well back into the nineteenth century.

The American influence in advertising may even be seen in circus ads. A large ad, which was obviously of American inspiration, appeared in the <u>Boletín Mercantil</u> urging the people not to miss the 'Gran Circo Americano de Roberto Stiekney & James Donovan'.[77] The Irishman must have refused to allow his name to be given the Spanish version.

In 1889 Spanish firms were advertising the fact that they were specializing in American products. This commercial exchange undoubtedly increased a desire to know the English language because even the <u>Boletín Mercantil</u> advertised that it was ready to sell a new English grammar that had just arrived from New York, "El Maestro de Inglés".[78] No matter how much that paper might disapprove of Americans and their way of advertising, it was always ready to accept the American dollar for advertisements.

It may be said that there was a marked influence exerted by the American press upon the Puerto Rican press between the years 1888 to 1898 in advertising. European advertisements remained much the same during that period, but Puerto Rican commission agents who represented American firms were affected by American methods. There was a variety in the presentation of their products that the European advertisement lacked. This, in the opinion of the writer, was due to the increased commercial relations between Puerto Rico and the United States and a respect for American business ability---in short, due to the American influence.

To summarize: the American press exercised a great influence on the Puerto Rican editor and his paper. That influence was shown in Puerto Rican columns in many ways, ranging from expressions of admiration and envy to diatribes of hate and ridicule. This reaction was seen especially in Spanish-

American relations concerning Cuba. A great emphasis has been given to Cuba and American intents and purposes regarding that Pearl of the Antilles, sometimes to the apparent neglect of Puerto Rico. However, it must be remembered that in the minds of the Spanish government and of the people of Cuba and Puerto Rico those two Antilles were regarded as one. What ever happened to Cuba could not but have a direct influence upon the future of Puerto Rico. This was true in commercial treaties, the probability of autonomy, and the outcome of any revolution---thus the great concern for everything that the American press said about Spain or her possessions. As sources of information, as models, or as scapegoats, the American newspapers played a prominent part in the Puerto Rican press.

(1) El Clamor del País, April 8, 1893.
(2) El Clamor del País, August 18, 1892.
  La Correspondencia de Puerto Rico, October 30, 1895; November 22, 1897; January 26, 1898.
  El País, August 24, 1897.
  La Razón, October 23, 1890.
  El Buscapié, May 17, 1894.
  El Eco, June 18, 1896.
  The conservative point of view was presented by the Boletín Mercantil, September 16, 1888; March 6, 1889; February 21, 1890; July 26, 1891; March 27, 1896.
(3) El Buscapié, November 17, 1889.
  La Correspondencia de Puerto Rico, December 29, 1890 and El Clamor del País, July 28, 1888 agreed with El Buscapié.
(4) El País, February 16, 1897.
  El Clamor del País, August 20, 1891.
  Even the conservative Boletín Mercantil, June 16, 1889, recognized this spirit in the American press.
(5) Boletín Mercantil, April 11, 1888; February 13, October 11, 1889; August 22, 1890.
(6) El Diario de Puerto Rico, April 1, 1894.
(7) La Democracia, March 20, 1895.
  La Razón, March 25, 1890.
  El Clamor del País, January 3, 1894; August 18, 1892.
  El Diario de Puerto Rico, July 17, 1893.
(8) El País, December 19, 1896.
  El Buscapié, October 23, 1895.
(9) Boletín Mercantil, May 24, 1889; August 22, 1890; November 30, 1890; January 22, February 8, 1893; May 31, 1893.
  La Balanza, May 24, 1893.
  La Razón, August 28, 1890.
  El Buscapié, August 31, 1890.
(10) Boletín Mercantil, May 27, 1888.
(11) La Correspondencia de Puerto Rico, April 21, 1898.
  Boletín Mercantil, August 25, October 2, 1889; January 22, 1893; September 20, 1896.
(12) El Clamor del País, December 3, 1889.
(13) El Clamor del País, April 11, 1891.
  The Boletín Mercantil found this an opportunity to attack liberty and democracy in the United States in its numbers of April 19, 29, May 6, 1891; May 20, 1892; May 26, 1895.

(14) El País, December 29, 1896; June 26, 1897.
El Buscapié, October 31, 1896.
La Correspondencia de Puerto Rico, October 5, 1895.
(15) El País, June 25, 1896.
Boletín Mercantil, July 25, November 28, 1888; August 7, 1892; October 18, 1895; March 8, 1896.
(16) El País, May 22, 1897.
El Buscapié, April 11, May 22, October 18, 30, 1895.
La Correspondencia de Puerto Rico, March 5, 1896; June 7, 1897.
(17) Boletín Mercantil, June 21, 1896.
El País, July 10, December 18, 1896.
La Correspondencia de Puerto Rico, April 8, 1895.
(18) Boletín Mercantil, May 1, 1891.
(19) El Diario de Puerto Rico, July 24, 1893.
Boletín Mercantil, May 19, December 31, 1893.
La Correspondencia de Puerto Rico, May 31, 1893.
(20) Boletín Mercantil, February 17, 1889; November 11, 1891.
El Buscapié, October 2, 1896.
La Correspondencia de Puerto Rico, October 5, 1895.
(21) Boletin Mercantíl, September 16, 1888; January 22, 1893; April 17, 1896.
La Correspondencia de Puerto Rico, February 10, 1893.
El Buscapié, October 31, 1895.
(22) Boletín Mercantil, July 26, 1893.
(23) El Buscapié, June 4, 1896.
Boletín Mercantil, March 29, 1896.
La Correspondencia de Puerto Rico, August 9, October 25, 1897.
La Democracia, April 18, 20, 1898.
El País, December 29, 1896.
(24) Revista Mercantil, March 28, 1895.
El Buscapié, June 15, 1896.
La Correspondencia de Puerto Rico, October 27, 1897.
(25) Boletín Mercantil, May 19, 28, June 18, July 26, December 31, 1893.
La Correspondencia de Puerto Rico, May 31, July 17, 1893.
El Buscapié, May 21, 1893.
La Balanza, May 19, May 31, June 21, 1893.
El Clamor del País, May 4, 1893.
(26) Boletín Mercantil, November 5, 8, 1893; March 30, 1894.
(27) El Buscapié, February 28, 1892.
Boletín Mercantil, July 1, 1888; November 3, 1891; January 24, 1897.
(28) Boletín Mercantil, May 11, March 20, September 16, 1888; January 8, 1890; February 22, May 1, 1891; March 11, 1898.
La Democracia, September 23, 1897.
(29) Boletín Mercantil, January 4, 1888; April 10, 1895; March 24, April 1, 1898.
(30) Boletín Mercantil, June 8, 1888.
El País, October 25, November 17, 1897; March 22, 1898.
La Correspondencia de Puerto Rico, October 27, 1898.
La Balanza, March 29, 1893.
El Buscapié, May 7, 1896.
(31) Boletín Mercantil, July 19, 1891.
(32) Ibid, August 12, 1891.
(33) Boletín Mercantil, August 12, 1891; January 22, 1893; December 29, 1895.
El País, March 25, 1896.
La Democracia, November 3, December 15, 24, 1896; November 15, December 11, 1897.
La Balanza, January 20, February 8, 1893.

(34) Boletín Mercantil, November 30, 1888; June 7, 1895.
El Buscapié, October 8, November 21, 1896.
La Balanza, March 29, 1893.
El Clamor del País, May 25, 1893.

(35) El Buscapié, May 11, 1896.
El País, July 2, 1896.
La Correspondencia de Puerto Rico, October 26, 1892; April 14, 1898.
La Democracia, July 31, 1896.
Boletín Mercantil, March 16, 1890; March 23, 1898.

(36) Boletín Mercantil, May 26, 1895; August 5, 1892.
La Correspondencia de Puerto Rico, August 22, October 30, 1895.

(37) Boletín Mercantil, April 14, 1895.

(38) La Correspondencia de Puerto Rico, March 15, 1895; October 30, 1895.
El País, May 11, 1897.
El Buscapié, May 21, 1893.
Boletín Mercantil, January 8, April 3, August 5, October 23, 1892; May 26, 1895; October 23, 1896; June 13, July 2, 1897.

(39) Boletín Mercantil, June 21, 1895.

(40) Boletín Mercantil, May 20, November 28, 1888; February 17, 1889; May 31, 1895; April 14, 1895.
La Correspondencia de Puerto Rico, April 8, 1895; December 2, 1896.

(41) El País, January 3, 1896.

(42) La Correspondencia de Puerto Rico, July 25, 1895; January 2, July 15, 1897.
La Democracia, October 2, 1897.

(43) La Correspondencia de Puerto Rico, March 16, 1895.
La Democracia, March 28, 1895; October 2, 1897.
Boletín Mercantil, January 8, 1892; January 26, 1898; March 11, 1898.

(44) El Liberal, March 9, 1898.

(45) El País, December 19, 1896.

(46) El Buscapié, December 5, 1896.
El País, October 28, 1896.

(47) Boletín Mercantil, March 20, July 1, 25, November 29, 1888; May 26, 1895; October 23, 1896.

(48) La Correspondencia de Puerto Rico, March 21, 1895.
La Democracia, November 23, 1897.
Boletín Mercantil, March 11, 1896.

(49) La Correspondencia de Puerto Rico, March 5, 1898.
Boletín Mercantil, June 21, 1897; January 28, February 18, March 11, April 1, 1898; January 24, 1897.
El País, March 24, 1898.

(50) El País, December 29, 1896.

(51) Boletín Mercantil, January 28, 1898.

(52) Ibid.

(53) La Balanza, March 10, 1893.
Boletín Mercantil, February 3, 5, January 22, 1888; September 23, November 3, 1893; December 21, 1894; July 11, August 18, September 6, 1895.
La Correspondencia de Puerto Rico, December 2, 1896.

(54) Boletín Mercantil, July 20, 1890; November 3, 1891; February 26, 1893; February 19, March 13, 27, September 6, 1896.
El Buscapié, May 13, 1895.
La Pequeña Antilla, January 15, 1896.

(55) Boletín Mercantil, November 30, 1888.

(56) <u>Boletín Mercantil</u>, June 19, 1889.
(57) <u>Ibid</u>, April 3, 1891. Similar articles appeared in numbers of April 4, 1888; September 2, 1890; June 8, 1894; March 8, 27, 1896; July 2, 1897. <u>El País</u>, March 8, 1897 also had an article in the same vein.
(58) <u>El Clamor del País</u>, August 27, 1892.
(59) <u>Boletín Mercantil</u>, January 23, February 18, 1898.
(60) <u>Boletín Mercantil</u>, March 2, 11, 13; April 3, April 20, 1898. <u>La Correspondencia de Puerto Rico</u>, April 13, 1898. <u>La Democracia</u>, January 26; February 21, 23; March 18, 1898.
(61) <u>Boletín Mercantil</u>, March 11, 13, 1898.
(62) <u>Ibid</u>, April 1, 1898.
(63) <u>El País</u>, March 24, 1898. <u>Boletín Mercantil</u>, April 20, 1898.
(64) <u>El Liberal</u>, March 9, 1898.
(65) <u>Boletín Mercantil</u>, April 1, 1898. Other reports of a similar nature are found in <u>El País</u>, July 31, 1896. <u>El Buscapié</u>, February 28, 1892. <u>Boletín Mercantil</u>, April 10, 1895.
(66) <u>La Democracia</u>, April 6, 11, 1898. <u>Boletín Mercantil</u>, March 13, 1898. <u>La Correspondencia de Puerto Rico</u>, April 19, 1898. <u>El Liberal</u>, March 17, 1898.
(67) Labra, Rafael María de, <u>La Reforma política</u>, p. 737.
(68) <u>Boletín Mercantil</u>, July 5, 1889; July 24, 1896. <u>El País</u>, January 7, 1897.
(69) <u>El Clamor del País</u>, January 19, 1894. <u>El Buscapié</u>, June 21, 1891; January 7, 1894.
(70) <u>Boletín Mercantil</u>, May 1, 1895.
(71) <u>El Buscapié</u>, June 21, 1891.
(72) <u>El Clamor del País</u>, January 19, 1894.
(73) <u>El Clamor del País</u>, February 18, 1893.
(74) <u>Ibid</u>, February 9, 1888.
(75) <u>Boletín Mercantil</u>, January 30, 1891.
(76) <u>La Razón</u>, May 22, 1890.
(77) <u>Boletín Mercantil</u>, May 13, 1892.
(78) <u>Ibid</u>, February 28, December 12, 1888; November 1, 1889; May 21, 1890; August 13, 1890.

American Politics

American politics and politicians have always been considered unique, sensational, vulgar, and fascinating by the foreigner. Thus were they described by the Puerto Rican press no matter what the political belief of the particular paper. An outsider's first sight of torchlight parades, giant barbecues, and baby-kissing, glad-handing, cigar-passing American politicians was something never forgotten. It was felt that the American politician who wished to be popular had to make a profession of simplicity and commonness. According to an insular paper he had to feign many things: simplicity in all his official acts, carelessness in dress, gallantry, lack of education, and respect for religion. Such requisites were not understood by foreign readers. Those seemed to be the universal requirements of an American president, whether a Lincoln, a Cleveland or a Bryan. It was the will of the majority and the majority had to be obeyed.[1]

The Puerto Rican correspondent or tourist recorded faithfully the most minute detail of the great American spectacle---the election. Nevertheless, the insular papers tried to analyze American elections as expressions of national sentiment. Sometimes they succeeded in doing so; other times their deductions were a little bizarre.

Some papers tried to estimate American politics. El País rather disconcertedly realized that for one reason or another the party in power seemed to lose its prestige in the United States. Questions on which depended the prosperity and integrity of the republic appeared to arise just after elections. In 1860, when the Democrats lost, the slave question presented itself and the Civil War resulted. In 1885, when the Democrats returned to power, political corruption was so great that no conclusion could be drawn regarding loss of prestige. However, division in the Democratic ranks brought about the Republican victory of 1888. Those protectionists imposed the McKinley Bill and thus created an anti-American sentiment in Europe. The period of deficits began with their wasting of money and the reckless bestowal of pensions to war veterans; this combination of causes brought about the Democratic victory of 1892. Again the Democrats played in bad luck. Their lack of cohesion, the unbalanced budget, the rapid depreciation of silver, and the Panic of 1893 all brought about the return of the Republicans in 1896. McKinley interpreted the situation as being one above partisanship, a crisis more important than that of 1860. The effort then had been directed toward the saving of the Union. In 1896, he said, the country was united and the main effort was the maintenance of the financial honor of the nation. He derided the idea that the country had no confidence in itself; that was ridiculous because the monetary situation transcended political groupings. All of this was simplified by El País. The paper believed that the fight was not merely a monetary one but that it had become sectional, that it was a case of opposition between the farmers and the industrialists, between the South and the West against the East. In other words, the poor had declared war on the rich, the Democrats had divided and the majority of them had abandoned the principles of Jefferson. No longer did those principles play the dominant part. The real and vital part was now being played by new tendencies, tendencies as illustrated by the socialistic ideas of Bryan.[2]

American political platforms disturbed Puerto Rican editors, especially if those platforms had anything to do with insular products. The fact that the Republican party favored a highly protectionist platform was viewed with alarm. McKinley was perhaps the most unpopular individual American in Puerto Rico for that very reason. Republican platforms uniformly condemned the Democratic policy of favoring reciprocity treaties. The American desire for self-sufficiency was not understood very well. When the various planks read that the foreign policy of the United States should be energetic, strong, and honorable, that Hawaii should be annexed, the Danish islands bought for naval bases, the Nicaraguan Canal constructed, and the influence of the United States maintained throughout the world, Puerto Rican editors began to doubt democratic sincerity. References to the maintenance of the Monroe Doctrine and friendship for the Cuban rebels were sure to ignite the rather easily inflamable Latin temperament. Americans are accustomed to political platforms that in themselves are nothing more than platitudes. Politicians can favor prosperity as a plank and get away with it. Of course in times of depression something more to the point is necessary but usually political platforms are regarded as more or less amusing hocus-pocus to beguile the voters. Such declarations to the effect that the Republicans were following with interest the fight of the Cuban patriots against cruelty and oppression, that they wished the rebels success, and that the United States should use its influence to give independence to Cuba shortly were regarded with misgivings by the conservatives and with hope by the liberals. [3] Political phrases and words like 'shortly' and 'to follow with interest' were accepted to mean action in the immediate future. When the Democrats followed with similar declarations in their platform, [4] it seemed clear that the United States was a militant nation and determined to create a sphere of influence in the Western Hemisphere for itself.

It was felt that the expansionist tendencies of the new democracy were growing daily. The silver question as interpreted by Bryan in the Democratic platform was regarded as radical both economically and socially. The factory workers in the West (whom the Puerto Rican editors considered to be living in abundance already) flocked to the silver standard, to the alarm of conservatives in Puerto Rico. It was prophesied that the only ones who would gain from such a plank would be the demagogues and the speculators but certainly not the factory workers. Republican protectionism did not attract the attention of the latter. Nor did protectionism hold any attraction for sugar growing countries like Puerto Rico, so Puerto Ricans looked upon such platforms apprehensively. Populism was distrusted in Puerto Rico. When it appeared that the Democrats and the Populists would unite, foreigners were undecided as to which party to favor, Democratic radicalism or Republican protectionism. By favoring the political platform of the former it might indirectly encourage radicalism in Puerto Rico; by favoring the latter platform it would be working against the economic interests of the island. [5] It was argued that a man like Bryan would have on his side the anarchists and radicals and that this demagogic element would soon bring about a civil war which might be the signal for radicals in Latin America. [6] What were the Puerto Ricans to favor?

The silver mine owners of the West were convinced of the necessity of invading the enemy camp of the partisans of gold in order to win over the working classes there. Bryan spoke in Madison Square Garden but under the insuperable difficulties of an enormous auditorium, a great throng of people, and the terrific summer heat of New York. Everyone expected to hear the golden voice of the silver crusader. The great disillusionment of the crowd, according to the Puerto Rican correspondent in New York, was due to the fact that he read his speech instead of speaking extemporaneously. The New York fiasco rather heartened Puerto Ricans, who had felt that once Bryan invaded the East all would be over with logic and common sense and the rabble would be assured of the government. [7]

The Cuban question as discussed in American platforms played a prominent part in the Puerto Rican press. The various candidates after 1895 all had a paragraph expressing sympathy for Cuba and its struggle.[8] This was magnified to mean intervention of some kind. The reactionaries could point out how Puritanism had been transformed into Machiavellianism of the first water. Both parties were reported to be seeking Cuban votes with this slogan "North American Cubans, help us win, and if we win, Cuba will be free."[9] That seemed to be the best proof of the low character of American politics to the 'incondicionales'. Naturalized Cubans were regarded as dangers to Spain by the conservative Puerto Rican press. Their numbers and influence was greatly exaggerated and liberal papers had to point out the infinitesimal influence that thirty thousand Cubans could have upon an election where seventy million people were involved. It was natural for the conservatives to regard the Cubans as intruders in the United States and also as traitors to Spain. They even went so far as to say that those thirty thousand Cubans scattered about the United States were decisive in the election of McKinley and the defeat of Bryan and that they would influence the American people to regard as an enemy any president hostile to Cuban independence. This, said La Democracia, was foolish. The prestige and public opinion of the American government and nation was not formed that way. Magistrates in the American nation, continued the paper, were never the enemies of the people nor were the people the enemy of their elected president. Elections were regarded as accomplished facts to be rectified not by revolution but by the next election. Everyone went back to work when the election was over and soon forgot about the campaign. The idea, then, that thirty thousand Cubans could influence the people of the United States to remove a president if he did not work for the immediate independence of Cuba was regarded as fanciful by the paper. It was not the American way.[10]

Nominating conventions with their uproar was something ill understood by conservatives and liberals alike. It was asked how democracy could operate in the confusion and mob spirit of the nominating convention. The nomination of Bryan was an illustration. It was incomprehensible how a poor, young lawyer like him could swing the nomination. Everyone asked "Who is this Bryan?" Bryan's nomination was a complete surprise to the Puerto Rican editors and to people who were accustomed to seeing the 'right' thing done by the 'right' people. To be of that 'right' group one had to be influential, wealthy, well-known, conservative to a degree, and well past middle age. Bryan had none of those qualifications. Outside the United States no one knew the man. He had been making on the average of two dollars per day in Lincoln, Nebraska, according to reports.[11] His radicalism was prover beyond a doubt. Many thought him to be in league with the devil or at least with the anarchists, which was just as bad.[12] The fruits of his nomination were immediate, as many Eastern Democrats refused to follow this new Moses. They renounced their party and went over to the Republicans. This action, to people impressed with the solidarity of the two party system of the United States, seemed indicative of a coming revolution. The 'arch-anarchist', Atgelt, went over to Bryan and this seemed to show that democracy had ceased to exist. The tried and true Republican East, the home of constitutional traditions, was now to be invaded by demagogues, agrarians, and miners. Perhaps the next thing that would happen would be that the artisans and factory workers would join this radical movement.[13] Bryan's chances were regarded as equal with those of McKinley. It was pointed out that he had the support of the Populists, Tammany Hall ("the most corrupt political organization in the United States"), the silver Republicans, the agrarian West, the solidly Democratic South, and the free silverites. That was felt to be an almost invincible organization. The economist and writer,

Henry George, was quoted as having said "the people of the United States want a speaker rather than an administrator". On the day of Bryan's successful nomination some typical Yankee political scenes took place. Displays of marital devotion in public (Latins have never approved of this), Bryan's statement that he always carried a lucky rabbit's foot, the congratulation of the successful candidate by crowds of politicians were all typically American and commented upon as such in the Puerto Rican press.[14] The first official act of the nominee was to repudiate Cleveland and his policy and to proclaim himself as the successor of Jefferson.

One paper attempted to analyze an American election. In the regime of electoral freedom that the United States enjoyed, the paper stated that it was true that the public, like so many cattle, theoretically, could be driven one way or the other. Therefore, if one were to follow that deduction to its logical conclusion, the election in question in the United States could not be considered as a true expression of the national will. But, it continued, that would be to apply European parliamentary and electoral systems to the United States and that was unjust. It was true that the European electoral system was vitiated to the extent that the party in power could perpetuate itself almost indefinitely by bribery or trickery. That was not the system followed in the United States, according to the article. In the American election, that event could be considered as an expression of the spontaneous feeling of the whole country. In 1890 the nation was not in accordance with the way that the Republican party had been running the country. An election was held and that party defeated. Some people might have attributed that defeat to the Populist party that was able to control the farm vote, or the McKinley Bill that made so many people angry, or the use of foreign money to influence the people and to buy votes in order to throw out the party known for its high tariff, selfish protectionism, and opposition to anything foreign. El Buscapié believed that the foreigner, accustomed to the working of the European parliamentary system, would have chosen any one of those reasons for the Republican defeat, but the paper maintained that the real reason was the solemn protest of the people as expressed in the ballot boxes. The sudden repudiation of the Republicans surprised the European and even the American voters. This action was hard to understand in countries where the government, instead of being the tool of the people, made the people its tool. There the government had at its disposal influence, resources, secrets, the national treasury, force, and the law. How could the Republicans have allowed such a thing to happen?[15]

Elections were an old story to the 'constitutional' governments of Europe. There the governments elected themselves beforehand and prepared their majorities and triumph. An election meant that industries might have to stop work if the voting, by some miracle or coup d'etat, were adverse to the party in power. If that happened the country would be on the verge of revolution, riots would occur, conditions would be such that all ordinary business would have to cease until the situation improved, and scandal would succeed scandal until force would be required to solve the matter. In contrast the American people seemed to have progressed a little farther with its interpretation and practice of constitutional government.

It was observed that an overturn in an American election did not fill the people with surprise. A revolution of ideas might occur in the United States without an armed revolution, with moral and poli ical degradation, and without governmental persecution of opponents. A government might be uprooted simply because the voters were dissatisfied with it. This, according to El Buscapié, was an admirable example worthy of the applause of the world. The paper went on to prophesy the future president of the

United States. The Republicans, it said, were finished for the present. No matter how they might try to buy votes or what combinations or political formulas might be used, the next president would be a Democrat because the people had spoken in the Congressional election of 1890. A change in foreign and domestic policy was envisaged. All that the Democrats had to do was to be worthy of public favor.[16]

That kind of reasoning was sure to set the Boletín Mercantil off on a diatribe under the general heading of "All that glitters is not gold" or "Facts will tell". The facts in reference were those of the manipulation of votes, and the bribery, frauds, and scandals associated with the stuffing of ballot boxes. The Boletín and other rightist papers urged its readers not to be duped by the so-called electoral sincerity and honesty of the United States. Those, they said, were merely glittering generalities which operated more in theory than in practice. One had only to read articles from the New York Post, the conservatives said, in order to learn about the illegalities of American elections.[17]

A certain cynicism prevailed in Puerto Rico concerning lobbies and pressure groups in American politics. Latin politics have always been characterized by those appendages of democracy. Being of a 'good' family can be ranked with being a member of a pressure group. In Congress every tariff bill was productive of wrangling, which could easily bring about a rupture of commercial relations between Spain and the United States. The trusts were believed to have contributed a great deal of money for the elections for the purpose of protecting their interests. The accusation of the president and the press that the trust had bribed senators to vote against making sugar a free article seemed to belie American democracy. A certain cynicism, then, pervaded Latin thoughts whenever trusts were involved with the government. Legislation, it was felt, was sure to be against Puerto Rico and favorable to the trust. The fate of the anti-trust laws was compared to the fate of cholera victims.[18] Sugar legislation was sure to be delayed until the moment when the trust was sure of victory. Anti-trust laws which would affect sugar interests would somehow be struck with that political cholera that made all action sluggish and weak until the time came when the trust could defeat those laws.[19]

It was realized that many political speeches exaggerated, mainly for the purpose of getting votes. The theatrical declarations of the Republicans during Cleveland's presidency were correctly evaluated by the Puerto Rican press. Sherman was on the Committee of Foreign Affairs at that time. In that position his words had an importance that those of other senators lacked. The Cubans could take heart when that man made a pronouncement concerning them although he would invariably be in the minority when a party vote was taken. As Secretary of State the conservatives feared that he would put into operation the views that he had expressed while making speeches to embarrass President Cleveland.[20]

Conservatives described the United States during elections as a battlefield where the contending parties employed all sorts of resources in order to win. Votes were bought, politicians were bribed, and while the campaign was going on and the election being decided the nation was in a state of chaos.[21] The fact that the nation abruptly dropped politics and turned to business as soon as the election was over was short of amazing. Some Puerto Ricans felt that during an election all the rights of citizens were violated and that the will of the voters was thwarted by unscrupulous propagandists. This was pictured to be more true of presidential elections than of any other. Untrue portraits of the opposing candidates were painted by

the enemy propagandists while their own candidate was lauded to the skies.
Shootings, scandals, and persecutions to convince the voters to vote the
right way were reported graphically by the conservative papers.[22] If those
methods did not work there were always falsification of voters' lists, the
abolition of districts, partisan newspapers, bands, cigars, flowers, and beer
in great quantities to rely upon.[23] Elections were pictured by the 'incondicionales' as gatherings of drunkards where the biggest business was the
buying of votes. Naturally, the purpose of this was to convince the liberals
that they were looking to the wrong country as a model, that the real country to admire was Spain and not the United States. Examples of violence
were cited with that purpose in view. It was shown that the election of Gar-
field had been one of the most violent in the history of the Union and that it
had a logical conclusion---the assassination of the president. Were all
these briberies, brawls, frauds, and violence with their legacies of hatred
commensurate with the so-called liberties of the model republic?[24] Even
the sanctity of Cleveland's home had been attacked by his opponents. To
the Latin, there could be no better proof of the disgusting methods that the
democratic politicians would use.[25] The operations of Tammany were cited.
Crusades for political morality in New York City were proven to be just so
much wasted effort.[26] Always, whenever an especially violent diatribe was
printed in the Boletín, the editor would say that he did not invent nor speak
just to be speaking but that he was merely relating all the news that he had
received from the United States. He who doubted could consult the North
American press.[27] All that had been implied, then, was a solid proof that
perfection was not of this world in spite of the fact that many admirers of
the United States believed that nation to be the model republic.[28]

Elections in the Yankee democracy, to the conservatives, were indications of the disagreeable rise of the middle class. As a result men of
intelligence and ability were not chosen for high positions. Demagoges and
men of materialistic spirit rose to power while men of character never had
a chance. "Arkansas Bills" were severely judged.

The liberal papers could point out that justices of the state supreme
courts received the same punishment as ward-heelers if they violated
American electoral laws. One such example was cited of a justice who had
used his judicial office to influence the voters illegally. Now, the paper
concluded triumphantly, the justice had plenty of time in jail to rue his action and to remember now that he was living in Uncle Sam's house.[29]

The Puerto Rican reaction to American politics was that in general
the Yankees knew how to accept philosophically the accomplished fact of
the election. Political assassinations were the fewest in that country where
lynchings seemed to abound.[30] After the election, everyone, Democrats
and Republicans alike, waited patiently for the next presidential election in
order to register their approval or disapproval of the party in power. In
the meantime, everyone was re-building his political fences in districts
where they were the weakest. He did that by appealing to the country in
various ways. Democrats would point out the beauties of free trade and
Republicans would show that protection was the best policy in the world.[31]

European papers, as quoted in the Puerto Rican press, predicted an
era of more liberal trade relations between Europe and the United States
with every Democratic victory.[32] The press, economists, and financiers
of the Old World usually restricted their comments to economic matters
when dealing with American elections.[33] Ideology was seldom considered
unless it had a direct bearing on economics.[34] Harrison's plan to annex
Hawaii meant American imperialism, a thing which European countries

considered to be an exclusive European product; Cleveland's defense of Venezuela was thought to be the first step of the expulsion of Europe from the New World; Bryan was a monetary threat to European financial dominance;[35] McKinley meant recalcitrant protectionism and the exclusion of European products from the United States. The fact that any one of those men might be morally right did not matter. In the opinion of El País and La Correspondencia de Puerto Rico, material interests alone guided European thoughts concerning American politics, politicians, and parties.[36]

The Puerto Rican reaction to American political platforms, campaigns, and elections was different from the European. Ideology counted for a little more in a few Puerto Rican papers. Some of the super-patriots of the island insisted that Spain should have an immediate 'showdown' with the Yankees over Cuba. But other papers advised the government to proceed quietly and cautiously in order not to kill the sugar trade with the United States and plunge Puerto Rico into depression and misery without practical results. El País explained that the Yankees were Yankees and that the Puerto Ricans should consider all angles of the question before indulging in any demonstrations that would be harmful to the island. Such was the paper's estimate of Yankee political phrases like "to help our Cuban friends, if possible". The phrase "if possible", the paper pointed out could mean just about anything. Why, then, get unduly excited about such statements? Above all, the Yankees were businessmen first and politicians only during elections. Other papers, liberal and conservative, could vouch for that. The Yankees, it was believed, would never get involved in any imbroglio that would upset their trade and commerce. In addition, Spain had enough troubles with the Cuban War and should not provoke added difficulties for the Spanish people and finances.[37]

The American theory of "to the victor belong the spoils" did not seem consonant with American political ideals. The touted fair play of democracy in that respect appeared no different from the Spanish governor's appointment of Puerto Rican mayors. When it was reported that Mr. James J. Van Allen had donated fifty thousand dollars to the Democratic campaign fund and had stipulated that he expected to be named the ambassador to England, liberal editors were nonplussed by this operation of the "spoils system" in the model republic.[38] Later the correspondence between Van Allen and Cleveland was published. From that it was seen that Van Allen admitted of having made the donation which he considered a very natural political duty and expressed himself as being very surprised that it had been used against him. He had only acted from purely altruistic motives.[39] All of this bandying of words somehow failed to convince either the conservatives or liberals that the American "spoils system" was any different from the age-old Spanish system of "cortando el bacalao" (cutting the cod-fish).

It was felt that after such a campaign as that of 1896 sectionalism would be the dominant note of future American politics. The fury of the present campaign proved, according to the press, that the capital of the United States was in an unfavorable location. The interests of the West claimed that the capital should be established in a more central place, St. Louis for example. The papers went on to predict that due to the acrimonious McKinley-Bryan campaign the country would necessarily have to divide and would soon constitute two independent nations. This was explained on the grounds that the West had been developed exclusively through the initiative of the pioneers, the advance of adventure-loving people who had only known privation and struggle, and that those people would always oppose the people of the East. The East was accused of corrupting western interests and of impoverishing the West with the unfair sale of western agricultural products. Therefore, the press concluded, the people of the West wanted to elect a candidate of their own who would look out for their interests in governmental circles.[40]

When McKinley was elected, a conservative paper merely stated that the new president was McKinley, "the most stalwart protectionist and the author of that infamous tariff bill which has been so greatly censured both in and outside of the republic."[41] On the same day La Correspondencia de Puerto Rico evidenced a more reasonable attitude toward the new president. It speculated as to his attitude toward Cuba, since it was implied in his campaign that he would favor independence; declared that he favored the gold standard and a high tariff; and went on to say that thus far he had shown ability only in fighting for the tariff and asked whether he had any other abilities. The paper concluded its resumé with a reassuring sentence by saying that relations should improve because McKinley did not appear to be of "the warrior type".[42]

The "Lame Duck" session offered a respite to Spain in regard to Cuba. The Puerto Rican paper appreciated this but thanked the people of the United States for it, not the politicians. Those politicians who were merely waiting for their successors to arrive could do nothing. This situation, it was felt, was due to the restrictions imposed by the American form of government upon its legislators. This, for once, appeared as a saving grace because it granted Spain a breathing spell. The democratic form of government, thus, operated for the benefit of Spanish interests ˰ Cuba. On the other hand, public opinion could change the whole situation.[43]

The plans of committees and the resolutions of legislatures did much to make up the mind of the new president. The composition of those committees appeared unusual to Latin readers. One such committee was composed of the ex-governor of New York, a policeman, the owner of the New York Sun, and John Astor, the millionaire.[44] In the face of all that agitation the preceeding administration was looked back upon as a golden age. Now there was need for Cleveland's moderation and Olney's cold blood. The policy advised by the press was that the Spanish government should abandon immediately its attitude of uncertainty and adopt a firm stand. "Spain should act as a strong and proud nation."[45]

The election of 1896 was interpreted in still other ways by the Puerto Rican press. La Democracia stated that Cleveland with his moderate attitude and pacific policy had been a guarantee of peace. It believed that affairs were going to change radically with the victory of McKinley because everyone knew that he was an ardent protectionist, a nationalist, and a firm believer in the Monroe Doctrine.[46] La Correspondencia de Puerto Rico was not so much afraid of the political policies of McKinley as of the economic. After all, it said, the United States was an Anglo-Saxon nation and interested chiefly in prosperity. This particular paper realized the promises of the party platforms were seldom kept after a victory. Circumstances and not sentimentalism, the paper continued, dictated policies. Therefore, according to La Correspondencia, the fears of La Democracia were groundless. McKinley would continue the monetary status quo (as Bryan would not have done) and Spain must be on guard against Yankee economic penetration.[47]

It was reported that the Spanish government preferred McKinley to Bryan although most of the Spanish authorities disliked both candidates. The causes for that unhappy choice was the ultra-radical tendencies of the Democratic candidate. Many advised Spain to do its utmost to end the war in Cuba in the four months between the presidential election of 1896 and the

assumption of power of McKinley on March 4th, 1897. After settling the
Cuban affair the Spanish government should arm to the teeth so as to fore-
stall any future American intervention in Cuba. This was necessary because the Yankees would not avoid a war simply on account of temporary
unpreparedness or lack of confidence. The Yankees were the strongest
potentially and the most self-confident race in the world, according to the
liberal papers. The point emphasized was that if Spain would end the rebellion during the "Lame Duck" session and then rearm in a formidable
manner, the United States would weigh the situation and would place national
welfare on one side and political adventure on the other.[48] That, in the estimation of La Democracia, would decide the Yankees for peace. Spain, too,
should view the Cuban situation in much the same light. If she were unable
to impose peace in those four months, then she should be willing to accept
a decorous peace rather than to risk a repetition of the Ten Years' War.[49]

Presidential inaugurals were evaluated at what they meant to Spanish-
American mercantile relations. Cleveland's inaugural, for example, implied the beginning of a new era of trade relations.[50] Usually, inaugural
speeches were reproduced in full in the Puerto Rican press for that very
reason. The weather in Washington was described, the picture of the parade
was given, and the public acclamation of the new president was presented
for the benefit of the Puerto Rican reader.[51] Inaugural statements like Mc-
Kinley's to the effect that the United States would never enter a war before
having exhausted all means for peace were given much space in the Puerto
Rican papers. This was interpreted as an indication of the new president's
common-sense and seemed to show the fruits of Cleveland's honesty, Spanish diplomacy, and Olney's far-sightedness.[52]

Messages and speeches of the presidents usually have the vagueness
characteristic of politicians. The state of the Union is given in detail:
money and finance are discussed; references are made to politically important sections of the country; a better future is expected and prosperity
is just around the corner. All such topics usually appear in presidential
messages, political speeches, or Fireside Chats. In short, they are mostly
high sounding platitudes that could be construed any way. Controversial
points are avoided. President McKinley made such speeches in 1897 and
1898 and naturally referred to Cuba and the rebellion there. He mentioned
the sympathy that the American people had for the unfortunate in Cuba
(which could be interpreted to mean either the loyalists or the rebels), but
at the same time the impossibility of intervention was also emphasized. He
conditioned the 'necessity to act' upon the support and approval of the civilized world. The jingo press seized upon the literal interpretation of the
phrase, 'the necessity to act', and shouted that there was a necessity and
that Spain was about to declare war on the United States. The first step,
according to the jingoes, was to recognize the belligerency of the Cubans
because it was a just and a humanitarian thing to do. The second was to
intervene actively to restore order. These pronouncements were ridiculed
by the Puerto Rican papers of the conservative side. They said that the only
desire of the northern politicians was to make advantageous commercial
treaties with Spain.[53] Those manifestations by the jingoes, therefore, were
convenient threats to hold over the heads of the Spanish authorities. They
had the same feeling toward the United States as the old toward the young.
They were afraid that the political theories of the lusty young giant would
find a warm reception among the Puerto Rican liberals.

Events proved this fear well grounded for the liberals continued their
relentless attack upon Spanish reaction. They asked why government should
remain a closed corporation in the hands of the royal governor and a few

wealthy families while the United States set an example to the world in democracy. Both the United States and Puerto Rico, they continued, were parts of the Western Hemisphere. There was no reason, they believed, why one should be democratic and the other autocratic. It was their contention that politics and government should be in the hands of the people as was the case in the model republic. They agitated for a more liberal suffrage law, political control over the royal governor, and a representative assembly which would give Puerto Rico the kind of government it desired. All of those things, the liberals emphasized, operated successfully in the United States and could, if given a chance, operate in Puerto Rico.

One of the editors of El País, José Celso Barbosa, had a different view of the United States. Barbosa went to the University of Michigan and there studied medicine. According to his daughter, Pilar, he dreamed of the day when his country might be governed in the same way as the state of Michigan. He thought it necessary to impose an unconditional American ideal against the 'incondicionales' of Puerto Rico and it was with that purpose in view that he returned to his island. He felt a strong sympathy for the democratic system as a result of his contacts at the northern university and desired that his island should have liberal institutions similar to those enjoyed by the state of Michigan.[54]

Ideas such as these, however, merely confirmed what the 'incondicionales' had long suspected---that Puerto Ricans educated in the North returned to the island with dangerous thoughts. Consequently, all kinds of obstacles were devised to prevent American political theory from getting a foothold in Puerto Rico. The conservatives hoped to hermetically seal the island from any northern influence. They met autonomist agitation with repression and hoped for a return of the good old days of the 'Componte'. Their most powerful colleague in the United States was the pro-Spanish newspaper, Las Novedades of New York City, which, even in the land of democracy and freedom, was watched by the American government. This, in the eyes of the reactionaries, was tantamount to persecution and therefore excused their attacks on the Puerto Rican liberals.[55]

American government was defined by some as worse than useless. This was based on the fact that an American paper advocated the abolition of the House of Representatives since all that it seemed to do was to interrupt the legislation of the Senate. It was felt by many that the House was full of radicals and demagogues that spent most of their time in useless talk and in passing resolutions of belligerency in favor of the Cuban rebels.[56] Even the Senate came in for its share of criticism whenever Senator Call* made speeches for the annexation of Cuba. It was asked why the liberals of Puerto Rico favored a system that permitted such actions against a friendly power. Legislative brawls were played up as battles and appeared thus "Batalla de legisladores en los Estados Unidos."[57]

Many people in Puerto Rico were accustomed to turning their eyes to the United States as a model for a new Puerto Rican form of government. In glowing words they painted pictures of the beauties of North American institutions, almost enough to convert the most monarchical person, but not quite. The conservatives retorted that, unfortunately, the picture was not quite true, as anyone could see if he did not use rose-colored glasses.

---

* Wilkinson Call, 1834-1910; Senator from Florida, 1879-1897; one of the best hated Americans by the conservative press due to his many resolutions for the annexation of Cuba and the granting of belligerency to the Cuban rebels.

Suffrage, they said, was not an actuality and the public welfare was not the supreme law for the American government; the government of the United States was in reality inspired only by the welfare of the particular party in power. All its acts were for the purpose of trying to perpetuate its position for its own particular benefit.[58] Las Novedades was vigorously supported by the Boletín Mercantil on such a stand. It was agreed that the latent love of the Puerto Rican republicans for all things pertaining to the United States, together with their hate for all that pertained to Spain, was a real danger to the Mother Country.

The liberal feeling that certain American institutions were superior to the Spanish was especially evident in regard to the suffrage in the United States in comparison with the way that it operated in Puerto Rico. The Boletín ridiculed the sincerity of the American suffrage laws. It editorially castigated people who said that the Spanish government, politicians, and political parties should follow the example of the great republic in matters of suffrage, elections, and respect for the elector. However, acts speak louder than words. What good was suffrage in a country where frauds and violence characterized elections? reasoned the Boletín. All the liberals had to do, continued the paper, was to refer to any American election and they would see the error of their ways.[59] Autonomist commissions that went to Spain to argue for suffrage reforms were good material for scathing attacks by the above mentioned paper. It and the liberals regarded such actions as just another step toward independence or autonomy.[60]

La Integridad Nacional, directed by the reactionary Vicente Balbás, referred to suffrage in much the same way. Vincente Balbás liked universal suffrage in Spain where the individuals of the different parties worked together for the grandeur of Spain, but universal suffrage would not be good for Puerto Rico, he said, because the Puerto Ricans might get the idea of rebellion from it. The irrepressible liberal, Mario Braschi, replied to the contrary. He said that Puerto Rico would use universal suffrage better than any other province of Spain. He asked why it should cause panic to La Integridad Nacional when the Puerto Rican people were just as Spanish as any person in Spain. The tragedy to him was that Puerto Ricans went to the United States and realized how that country advanced under a liberal system while Puerto Rico went to ruin under the most absolute centralism, restricted rights, and one of the worst administrations in the world.[61] La Razón believed that the Puerto Rican political, economic, and financial system was all wrong. It felt that the Minister of Ultramar dallied and wasted his time with stupid projects like the conversion of the coinage and fantastic economic schemes while more vital problems remained unsettled. Those problems were the suffrage, which would make the people of Puerto Rico better satisfied with the Spanish administration, and better commercial treaties with the United States which would convince Puerto Ricans that the Spanish government paid some attention to insular problems. When Puerto Ricans were rated as third class citizens and therefore in an under-privileged position, La Razón believed that something should be done to satisfy insular complaints. The least that could be done, it felt, was a revision of the suffrage laws.[62]

Attacks on race prejudice and the operation of the American Congress were in order. Articles entitled "Excesos de libertad" were common. It was not understood how the president could permit legislators to speak against him in debate. Such actions should be followed by a jail term for the rash Congressman. Those politicians must lack education and dignity said the conservatives. That sad truth was revealed by the fact that the president had to veto about three hundred laws presented to him by the

Senate. It was felt by the reactionary press that everywhere there were people who abused freedom of speech but nowhere as in the United States. There existed the least respect for the constituted authorities and very little attention was paid to the duties of international courtesy.

Senator Tillman* accused President Cleveland of being a charlatan, a hypocrite, and a tyrant; declared that he issued bonds without authorization and sold them in secret and for that reason had corrupted his conscience with the bankers of Wall Street. That kind of language coming from a senator gave the excuse to foreign editors to use the same style when talking about the United States. When the senator attacked the corruption of the government and predicted that the United States was moving toward a system of government in which judicial decisions ruled in favor of monopolies and of the rich he was applauded by the anti-American press of Puerto Rico. Tillman also proposed that the millions of unemployed should go to Washington with rifles and recover in that manner the liberties that had been stolen from them. Senator Call spoke in much the same vein when he talked about the Spanish army in Cuba. He reported to the Senate that Spanish soldiers walked about the streets of Habana with Cuban babies impaled on their bayonets. Other nonsense of a similar nature and attacks like those of Senator Tillman did little to improve the conservatives' opinion of the United States.[63]

No matter what happened in the American Congress, one idea prevailed in Puerto Rico---that Yankee governmental agencies were fickle. Sometimes they adopted a reserved and conservative attitude and then suddenly changed to a rebellious and belligerent attitude. Some Puerto Ricans felt that the best way to settle the situation was for Spain to conquer the American capital and thus to end all bickering. That seemed to be the best policy as American political dissension appeared to invite intervention. El Buscapié suggested that the best cure for generals with those ideas would be to send them on a similar expedition some place in the world so that they could appreciate the difficulties of conquering the United States. Perhaps, then, they could get some idea of the distance between Washington and Chicago and would not be so anxious to imitate Napoleon's March to Moscow.[64]

American politicians, political parties, and platforms received different treatment from the Puerto Rican press according to the political faith of the paper. The press agreed on one thing which was that everything in the United States was markedly different from the same things in other countries. This was applied to politics with the resultant estimation that American politics were different from any other in the world. The antics of politicians seeking re-election, promises which were made so glibly just before the election and forgotten so blithely after the election, politicos who appeared for the moment and then were forgotten by an apparently ungrateful electorate were all characteristic of the American political scene in the eyes of the insular editor. Nothing seemed definite in that huge country because rules there seemed to be made just to be bro en. Nor did there seem to be any set rules for the political arena if one wer to judge by events. All was fair, Puerto Rican editors believed, in love and war---and American politics.

---

* Benjamin Ryan Tillman, U. S. Senator from South Carolina, 1894-1918. He was a bitter opponent of President Cleveland and a champion of a strong American navy. His violent anti-Negro attitude gained him national attention.

(1) Boletín Mercantil, November 29, 1896.
(2) El País, August 8, 24, 1896.
La Democracia, July 30, 1896.
(3) El País, July 27, 1896.
La Democracia, August 21, 1896.
Boletín Mercantil, June 21, 1897.
La Correspondencia de Puerto Rico, January 1, 1897.
(4) El País, July 31, 1896.
Boletín Mercantil, November 22, 29, 1896.
La Correspondencia de Puerto Rico, November 8, 1896.
(5) El País, August 24, 1896.
La Democracia, December 5, 1896.
La Correspondencia de Puerto Rico, November 5, 1896.
(6) La Correspondencia de Puerto Rico, November 8, 1896.
La Democracia, December 5, 1896.
El País, August 24, 1896.
(7) El País, September 18, 1896.
La Correspondencia de Puerto Rico, November 8, 1896.
La Democracia, November 5, 1896.
(8) El País, October 8, 1896.
La Democracia, July 31, August 21, October 10, 1896.
Boletín Mercantil, November 29, 1896.
(9) La Democracia, November 23, 1897.
Boletín Mercantil, August 28, 1888; November 25, 1896.
(10) La Democracia, November 9, 1896.
(11) El País, August 24, 1896.
Boletín Mercantil, November 14, 1896.
(12) El País, August 20, 1896.
Boletín Mercantil, November 22, 1896.
(13) El País, August 24, 1896.
Boletín Mercantil, August 20, 1896.
(14) El País, August 24, 1896.
Boletín Mercantil, November 29, 1896.
La Correspondencia de Puerto Rico, January 31, 1897.
(15) El Buscapié, December 7, 1890.
(16) El Buscapié, December 7, 1890.
(17) Boletín Mercantil, January 10, 1890.
La Balanza, February 26, 1893.
(18) Boletín Mercantil, September 21, 1894.
La Balanza, April 16, 1893.
(19) La Correspondencia de Puerto Rico, September 11, 1892.
El Clamor del País, March 3, 24, September 8, October 19, 1888
September 21, 1894.
Revista Mercantil, August 6, 1895.
Boletín Mercantil, March 23, 1888.
(20) La Correspondencia de Puerto Rico, January 31, 1897.
Boletín Mercantil, July 5, 1896.
(21) Boletín Mercantil, August 28, 1888; May 2, 1894.
(22) Boletín Mercantil, December 9, 1888; January 10, 1890.
La Balanza, March 6, 1893.
(23) Boletín Mercantil, November 29, 1896; November 3, 1895;
March 1, 1893.
La Balanza, August 11, 1892.
La Razón, November 6, 1890.
(24) Boletín Mercantil, August 28, 1888; December 9, 1888; January 10,
1890; January 31, March 11, 1894.
(25) Boletín Mercantil, December 9, 1888.

(26) La Correspondencia de Puerto Rico, April 4, 1893; December 18, 1893.
Boletín Mercantil, December 9, 1888; January 31, 1894.
(27) Boletín Mercantil, March 11, 1894.
(28) Ibid, December 9, 1888.
(29) El Diario de Puerto Rico, December 5, 1893.
Boletín Mercantil, March 11, 1894.
(30) La Razón, November 6, 1890.
El Buscapié, December 7, 1890.
La Democracia, November 9, 1896.
El Clamor del País, November 10, 1888.
(31) Boletín Mercantil, November 23, 1894; November 29, 1896.
(32) Boletín Mercantil, December 4, 1892.
La Democracia, July 30, 1896.
(33) Boletín Mercantil, December 4, 1892; October 22, November 22, 1896.
(34) El Pequeño Diario, March 23, 1895.
Boletín Mercantil, December 10, 1896.
La Democracia, July 30, 1896.
(35) El País, December 11, 1897.
La Democracia, December 5, 1896.
(36) El País, November 20, 1896.
La Correspondencia de Puerto Rico, December 8, 1896.
(37) El País, October 28, 1896.
Boletín Mercantil, June 21, 1897.
La Correspondencia de Puerto Rico, March 26, 1896.
(38) El Diario de Puerto Rico, April 10, 1894.
La Correspondencia de Puerto Rico, October 15, 1893.
(39) El Diario de Puerto Rico, April 10, 1894.
Boletín Mercantil, May 16, 1894.
(40) El País, August 24, October 8, 22, 24, 1896.
La Correspondencia de Puerto Rico, March 25, December 8, 1896.
(41) Boletín Mercantil, November 8, 1896.
(42) La Correspondencia de Puerto Rico, November 8, 1896
(43) La Correspondencia de Puerto Rico, January 5, 1897.
(44) Ibid, January 5, 1897; November 8, 1896.
(45) La Democracia, December 11, 1897.
La Correspondencia de Puerto Rico, January 5, 1897.
(46) La Democracia, November 5, 1896.
(47) La Correspondencia de Puerto Rico, November 5, 1896.
(48) La Democracia, December 5, 1896.
La Correspondencia de Puerto Rico, November 5, 8, 1896; December 8, 1896.
(The conservative Boletín Mercantil of November 8, 22, 1896, also urged intensive rearmament for the same reasons)
(49) La Democracia, December 5, 1896.
(50) Boletín Mercantil, December 9, 1892; April 7, 1893.
La Correspondencia de Puerto Rico, March 20, 1893.
(51) La Balanza, March 17, 1893.
Other newspaper accounts which refer to presidential inaugurals and speeches are:
Boletín Mercantil, December 11, 1897.
El País, November 18, 1897; October 25, 1897.
La Correspondencia de Puerto Rico, January 5, 1897.
(52) La Correspondencia de Puerto Rico, March 16, 1897.
(53) Boletín Mercantil, November 30, 1888; February 19, 1890; October 29, 1890; August 16, 1891; May 25, October 4, 1892; May 24, June 22, July 6, September 7, November 30, 1894.
La Balanza, March 19, June 4, 11, 1893.

(54) Barbosa, José Celso: <u>La Obra de José Celso Barbosa</u>, Vol. I, p. 24.
(55) <u>Boletín Mercantil</u>, May 11, 1888.
   <u>La Balanza</u>, October 13, 1893.
(56) <u>Boletín Mercantil</u>, February 8, 1890; February 28, March 6, 8, 29;
   April 12, June 21, October 18, 1896; June 11, 1897.
   <u>El País</u>, June 11, 24, March 5, April 9, 1896.
   <u>El Buscapié</u>, April 7, 11, 1895.
(57) <u>Boletín Mercantil</u>, June 8, 1894; March 6, 1896; June 11, 1897.
   <u>El País</u>, March 5, 1896.
   <u>El Clamor del País</u>, February 25, March 2, 1893.
(58) <u>Boletín Mercantil</u>, October 11, 1889.
   <u>La Balanza</u>, September 18, 1892.
(59) <u>Boletín Mercantil</u>, October 11, 1889; September 3, December 10,
   1890; June 24, 1891; March 27, 1896; July 21, 1897; February 20,
   1898. <u>La Balanza</u>, March 29, 1893, agreed with its conservative
   colleague.
(60) <u>El País</u>, January 4, 1897.
(61) <u>La Razón</u>, October 23, 1890.
(62) <u>Ibid</u>, October 25, 1890.
(63) <u>La Democracia</u>, February 4, April 6, 1898.
   <u>Boletín Mercantil</u>, February 5, 1893; March 27, 1896.
   <u>El País</u>, July 31, 1896; June 25, 1897.
   <u>La Balanza</u>, January 20, 1893.
(64) <u>El Buscapié</u>, April 6, 1896.

El Peligro Yanqui

The attitude of Puerto Ricans toward the Yankee peril usually followed party lines. Conservatives pointed to the Monroe Doctrine as a proof of the determination of the United States to maintain its hegemony in the Western Hemisphere. Liberals, on the other hand, made excuses for that doctrine and said that it was a New World protection against autocratic Europe. However, the Spanish authorities and their clique in Puerto Rico felt that such protection was detrimental to their interests. It was their belief that the principle of monarchy should be maintained and strengthened in the Antilles, in spite of what the United States or the Puerto Rican liberals might say.

Whenever a liberal paper disagreed with the aims of the Americans it was given much space in the conservative press. La Revista de Puerto Rico of Ponce attacked the American idea of Pan-Americanism. La Revista was thereupon praised by the Boletín for being a "discordant note in the so-called liberalism of Puerto Rico" where the larger part of those papers idolized "the democratic evidences of the United States and all that smells of the Yankee, even though he is one thousand miles away". The Boletín went on to attack the liberals by saying that for them the Yankee was divine, supreme, and without equal and that the long list of such offensive articles in the liberal papers was intolerable. The Yankees were said to be the Carthaginians of the nineteenth century. This was proven to the satisfaction of the reactionaries by many references to the Westward Movement. There in the West, they said, the Americans hunted the Red Man as though he were a wild beast, offering five dollars apiece for Indian scalps, which was comparable to the bounty paid for wolves in Spain. Now the Yankees were hunting the Latin-Americans with honeyed words in order to convert them into markets for the American manufacturers! The warning was clear. The Latins should avoid the net that the Yankees were spreading at Pan-American Conferences.[1]

Mariano Abril, the poet and historian, declared that as soon as the United States became powerful it became contaminated with the ambitions of old Europe. It abandoned its dedication to liberty and put on the helmet of the conqueror and began to crush that liberty which it once proclaimed. Thus the country of Washington and Lincoln became the modern Carthage of the New World. To Abril the tendency of the American nation appeared imminently dangerous. The American policy toward Spain seemed to indicate dissatisfaction with its role of an opulent merchant and its yearning to be a warrior in shining armor. The United States, during the era 1888 to 1898, appeared a nation in search of warlike adventure because of its designs on Hawaii and the Spanish Antilles. This was not in imitation of Don Quizote, who was filled with noble ideals, but more like the Carthaginians, to whom ambition had given strength for bold adventures. It was disillusioning to realize that America had suffered such a change. He sadly concluded that never in the history of humanity had people been moved by such ignoble ambitions as in the latter part of the nineteenth century.[2]

Diplomatic trouble between Spain and the United States was chronic and was given space in the papers of both countries. The Heraldo Madrid told about the incident of the American minister to Spain asking the Duke of Tetuán* to try to stop the language which the Spanish press generally

---

* Carlos O'Donnell y Abreu, 1834-1903; Spanish leader of Irish descent; Senator, 1876-1879; Vice-President of the Senate, 1881; Minister of State, 1895-1897.

used when it referred to American men or interests.[3] The Spanish minister in Washington had the same trouble in regard to Cuban autonomist papers and the yellow press.

The foreign as well as the domestic policy of the American political parties was discussed in detail by the Puerto Rican press. Discussion of American foreign affairs centered around the Yankee attitude toward the Caribbean area; that of domestic policy concerned the American tariff program. Did the United States aim for the hegemony of the Caribbean? If so, did that mean that European nations with colonies in the Western Hemisphere would be expelled?

Puerto Rican conservatives always answered in the affirmative; the liberals in the negative. The former felt that American nationalism and imperialism were on the rise. To them the Westward Movement, the fate of the Indians, the treatment of the negroes and Chinese, the Mexican War, and lastly (and the most important to the conservatives) American Cuban policy proved that the Yankees aimed at full political dominion in Latin America. Otherwise why had the United States tried to buy Cuba and the Danish islands?

American domination, according to the 'incondicionales', fell in two spheres: one, the political, which meant American ownership of the Caribbean islands; the other, the mercantile, which aimed at economic domination over the rest of Latin America. Both were condemned but the latter was considered the more insidious and, consequently, the more dangerous. There the Yankees were using the weapon they best understood---the dollar. It was a weapon, declared the conservatives, which Europeans could fight the least. Proud Spain, continued these Puerto Rican editors, had never been a money-grubbing nation with a mercantilistic foreign policy as was the Colossus of the North.

The liberals replied that American foreign policy was more high-minded than the picture presented by their opponents. If the United States intervened in Cuba it would be for one purpose only---that of liberating an oppressed people. A democratic people, said the liberals, was not interested in imperialism but in idealism.

By and large American foreign policy was judged in terms of political parties. Neither the Republican nor the Democratic party completely satisfied the Puerto Rican press in regard to that point. However, the insular editors were more inclined to take their chances with the Democratic interpretation of American rights and interests abroad than with the Republican.

They had good reason for this attitude, as they took pains to explain. Every injury to Spanish pride seemed to come during a Republican administration, whereas conciliation appeared during a Democratic. Had not the Republicans tried to annex Santo Domingo, Hawaii, and Cuba? President Harrison had almost annexed Hawaii, but his successor, Cleveland, nobly returned the island to its native queen. Democratic policy toward the Cuban revolt generally favored neutrality; Republican favored granting the status of belligerency to the rebels.

Republican foreign policy had been clearly outlined in their platform of 1896. It was friendship for the rebels and a desire for a speedy settlement of the Cuban question. No concessions could be expected from such a platform, especially when it was supported at the time by a strong pro-Cuban public opinion. Besides, McKinley was not deemed the kind of a man to pursue an independent policy. It was believed that if the party favored intervention in Cuba and Harrisonian imperialism he would bow to the dictates of the politicos.

Cleveland, during his administration, clearly demonstrated his independence of action. But that man had been repudiated by his party and a new leader, Bryan, was at the helm. What direction would this new man's foreign policy take? It was generally believed that Bryan would shove imperialism into the background and would concentrate on domestic affairs. The choice between McKinley and Bryan was difficult and the Puerto Rican editors were rather confused as to what man and what party best favored Antillean interests in 1896.

Some Puerto Rican papers attributed a Machiavellian cleverness and cunning to the United States in its Cuban policy. It was felt that the policy was a well planned system of pin-pricks, each one deeper than the last, until Spain would be on the verge of declaring war. Then conciliation would come, and after a prudent lapse of time, the procedure would begin again. Many Puerto Ricans believed this policy was calculated to lull the Spanish authorities into a state of false calm and security, based on the erroneous idea that the United States was a commercial and industrial nation, interested only in profits, peace, and prosperity; that its internal racial problems of the Indians, Chinese, and negroes would prevent any unified action in time of crisis; and that the independent actions of the jingo newspapers clearly illustrated that lack of governmental authority which would be doubly evident in a crisis. This wishful thinking on the part of Spain, so ably seconded by constant references to her past glories and victories, did much to continue the old procrastinating policy and the 'mañana' spirit.

One Puerto Rican paper explained the workings of such a system quite well. It said that whenever the New York Herald offended, the owner would send a satisfactory explanation to its Puerto Rican colleague and the matter was dropped. The same procedure was applied to American governmental activity. Whenever Spain heard about the Spanish minister's being insulted by a mob or an American judge's acquittal of some filibusters who had been caught red-handed, Mr. Taylor,[*] the American minister, would rush over to the Duke of Tetuan and say that it was all a joke and the matter would end in a toast to the amicable relations that had always existed between Spain and the United States.[4] As this procedure was repeated time after time, many editors became tired of this diplomatic fencing which seemed to do no one any good.

The question of Cuba became a dominant note in 1895. Along with reciprocal trade treaties, tariffs, and the monetary question, Cuba grew to be an integral part of American national politics. No matter what else happened in the Congressional or presidential elections, Cuba and its problems were always mentioned in some connection. It was feared that the return of a Republican to the presidency in 1896 would mean a revival of an aggressive foreign policy on the part of the United States. Therefore, the Puerto Rican papers warned their politicians to take notice and to be prepared for the worst, as the integrity of Spain was at stake. They said that if the Spanish statesmen had no solution of the Cuban problem to offer by the end of 1896, the American president with the full support of his party and country, would be ready to take any arbitrary action against the Spanish Empire. If those statesmen did not believe so, all they had to do was to recall the

* Hannis Taylor, 1851-1922; American author and diplomat; U. S. Minister to Spain, 1893-1897.

affair between Chile and the United States, which took place during a Republican administration. At that time, according to the version of El País, Blaine and Harrison had been ready to sacrifice Chile and to indulge in a war for the sake of a simple affair between some American sailors and some Chilean vagabonds. Next came Hawaii. Harrison had been ready to annex those islands at any cost. Now, the paper warned, the new president would be infinitely more dangerous than either Blaine or Harrison because of his past history as a protectionist, his animosity toward Spain, and the apparent mandate of the people and the party to do something to settle the Cuban problem. President McKinley would be inaugurated, it continued, in the turmoil of political passions which would begin to agitate immediately against Spain. There was no hope that McKinley would follow the modern policy of Cleveland. There was no hope for various reasons. The American press had not modified its attitude toward Spain, the American people were more partial to the Cuban rebels than ever before, and the political platform of the party gave no indication of a policy favorable to Spain. On the contrary, the party had expressed itself as being friendly with the rebels and hostile to the Mother Country. An alarming incident, in the eyes of the Spanish authorities, was the volunteering of cadets of an American cruiser to fight for the rebels against Spain. El País then passed to acid criticisms of the Spanish government, stating that it took little note of all those things because it lived in a world of imagination and dreams. The paper predicted that no concessions would be made by the United States to Spain, due to the inactivity of the Spanish ministers. That inactivity had placed the country in an indefensible position. Weyler* had issued a decree declaring that one month would be given American residents in Cuba to legalize their citizenship. That, according to the paper, would be productive of friction with the United States and would be another step toward war.[5]

La Correspondencia de Puerto Rico pointed out that public opinion in the United States during the "Ten Years' War", 1868-1878, and the Cuban revolt of 1895 was much the same. In both periods there had been movements to aid the rebels: committees urged all out aid to the Cubans and brought pressure to bear upon Congress to recognize the Cuban patriots, and Cuban bonds were issued. The paper added that the newspapers and the agitation of the two periods followed the same pattern. During both times, fortunately, there had been a president ready to apply common sense. In 1872 it had been Grant; in 1896, Cleveland. American politicians were shown to be the most practical in the world because happened either in 1872 or in 1896 to bring about a war between the United States and Spain.[6] And now the American policy of helping Cuba was felt to have a deliberate purpose, one which could only end with a conflict between the two countries. The United States was said to be taking advantage of Spain during the rebellion in order to appropriate all the commerce of the Caribbean.[7]

Throughout Cleveland's administration, however, the sensible of the Puerto Rican editors urged their readers to have confidence in the president and in Secretary Olney and their interpretation and enforcement of neutrality. Those men seem to have enjoyed great confidence in Puerto Rico---a greater confidence than was displayed towards them at times in their own United States.

---

* Valeriano Weyler y Nicolau, 1839-1930; Marquis of Teneriffe. Spanish soldier of Prussian descent; served in Cuba, 1868-1872; Captain-General of Canaries, Balearics, and Philippines. Followed a policy of stern repression and terror against the socialists of Catalonia in 1896 and against the Cuban rebels, 1896-1897. Minister of War, 1901-1902; Minister of Marine, 1905.

There were complaints against the Mother Country upon which both Cubans and Puerto Ricans agreed. The charges that the Puerto Rican Revolutionary Association brought against the Spanish government were: that Spain sent only the worst elements for governors, that no instruction other than the primary public schools was provided, and that the monetary system was humiliating and economically unsound.[8]

Autonomy for both the Antilles was suggested as a remedy for the situation. At the same time it was pointed out that the success of such a settlement would depend upon the sincerity with which Spain permitted a plebiscite and followed its decision. There was more than a slight intimation that the Spanish government would permit a plebiscite but would nullify the operation of autonomy with governmental obstruction and legal technicalities.[9] However, if autonomy were granted, it was admitted that this would be a powerful incentive for the Cubans to lay down their arms and would lessen the influence of the Revolutionary Juntas in New York. Such a concession, nevertheless, would have to be carried to completion by a man like General Martínez Campos* who was generally recognized to be honest. Many felt that the situation was complicated only to those who had an interest in making it appear so, but in the last analysis two things had to come: autonomy and General Martínez Campos.[10]

But the attitude of the United States was always considered in the granting of any reforms to the Antilles. The European nations with colonies in the Western Hemisphere, however, opposed any Spanish deference to the United States regarding Cuba and Puerto Rico. The majority of the European press in 1897, according to La Democracia, was hostile to President McKinley and his desire that the revolt be settled at once. The French were especially antagonistic toward the United States. La Democracia quoted a French newspaper's attack upon American conduct in the Antilles. It was felt that the United States was a young and aggressive nation which was looking for any opportunity to work off its excess vigor upon Spain. The Latin nations, according to the French paper, should band together under the leadership of France in order to defend Latin-Americanism against the Yankee Peril. There was the element of fear in this European attitude. The United States was an unpredictable factor in world politics and as such could not be trusted. Its affection for the Monroe Doctrine, its commercial penetration of the New World, and its great size were elements that inspired apprehension in the Old World powers. It was pointed out that the American speculators and politicians would not retreat in their attitude unless forced to do so. The force suggested was a European alliance of the nations that had colonies in the New World, an alliance which would be of such a character that even the rash and impetuous politicians of the United States would think twice in pursuing their Cuban policy.[11]

El País recognized the distrustful attitude of European nations interested in the Western Hemisphere. Nevertheless the paper derided the prognostications of the sages who prophesied that in the event of war Spain would not be alone. Those sages had pointed out that European nations would immediately rush to the assistance of Spain for many reasons. Their material interests and colonies and their aim of promoting European culture in the Western Hemisphere would serve to make them temporary allies. The

---

* General Martínez de Campos, 1831-1900; participated in the Moroccan war under General O'Donnell, in the Spanish intervention in Mexico in 1861 under General Prim, and in the suppression of the Cuban revolt of 1868-1878; an advocate of a just and liberal policy toward Cuba; a moderate liberal in Spanish politics.

supposed fear created by the strategic location of Spanish colonies throughout the world was also considered a reason for allies. First of all it was
pointed out that Spain was a warrior nation of Europe; lastly, that the Canaries and the Balearics were near England, the Philippines between England
and Japan, the Carolines between Japan and Germany, and Cuba and Puerto
Rico between the eyes of everybody. Those conditions, the sages proved,
would surround Spain with a circle of friends who would fight the United
States for various reasons---either to protect European colonies from the
Colossus or to keep in the good graces of Spain, a nation with so many strategic island-forts throughout the world.

The paper in question consigned this whole theory to the limbo of wishful thinking and asked the sages to consider one thing only before they in-
dulged in any more fantasies: the geographic position of the United States,
a factor which made the Colossus absolutely paramount in the West Indies.
Moreover, the economic dependence of the Spanish Antilles upon American
markets and foodstuffs was a reality which the Madrid strategists failed to
consider. Other realities that were disregarded were the war preparations
of the United States and the diplomatic advances of a Bismarckian nature
with which Uncle Sam was said to have made his debut into international
politics. "In the end", the paper concluded, "Spain and her colonies will
fight bravely but alone".[12]

The 'incondicionales' warned the liberals against the ulterior motives
of Uncle Sam in regard to Cuba. A strong warning at all times, if one were
to judge by the number of times that it was advanced, was the reference to
the race troubles of the United States. Surely the United States should not
want to aid a revolt whose principal characteristic was racism, even though
that racism was less violent than that in the Model Republic. Everyone,
said the conservatives, knew how the Indians, negroes, and Chinese were
treated in the United States. If they did not, all they had to do was to read
Uncle Tom's Cabin, which so graphically described the condition of the poor
negro in that country. Some motive, then, other than a humanitarian one
must be motivating the United States in interfering in Cuba.[13]

According to the conservatives, the intention of the United States in
the Caribbean was revealed in its quarrels with South American nations.
With every quarrel came an outburst of anti-American feeling. This expressed itself in multiple ways. The Monroe Doctrine was shown to mean
"America for the Yankees" and not "America for the Americans" (north
and south); the new American fleet was merely a portent of future aggres-
sion; and the ever present commercial penetration was demonstrated to
mean future political domination. However, with almost every outburst
there was a bit of advice at the end of the article to the effect that it would
be better to have a war of notes rather than one of the battlefield.[14]

The American peril, then, assumed many forms and was a constant
bugbear to the 'incondicionales'. Increased American naval strength, political platforms and parties, the jingo press, American books translated into
Spanish, Pan-Americanism, the Monroe Doctrine, and Yankee business and
commerce were all considered dangers to Spain in America. However,
there was one Yankee institution that held no threat for Spain. That was
the American Constitution. According to Don Rafael W. U. Ramirez, Professor of Puerto Rican History at the University of Puerto Rico, both the
Puerto Rican liberals and conservatives looked to Spain for guidance in
their discussions on constitutionalism. That situation was complicated because even the Spanish liberals could not decide whether they preferred a
unitary or a federal constitution and spent much time wrangling over that

question. The Peninsular conservatives, as might be expected, preferred no constitution at all, but if it had to come favored one whereby Madrid could legislate for the provinces. In that way the conservatives at the capital would control all of Spain instead of isolated provinces.*

The conservative press was fairly consistent in its conception of the Yankee peril. It felt that the Americanos were always thinking of extending their territory at the expense of the Latin-American nations in the way that they had marched westward at the expense of the Indians and Mexicans. With the examples of the fate which befell the Red Men, the Mexican Republic, and the Mormons it is small wonder that the conservatives were alarmed. They disagreed as to the exact method that the Yankees would use in their drive toward the south, but the majority believed that economic penetration would be succeeded by political domination. As a result, one of the great ideas of the conservative press was to promote Pan-Hispanism,** which would have a political, economic, and cultural foundation. However, due to the inability of the Mother Country to assimilate Antillean products, the continuance of anti-Spanish feeling in many of the Latin-American republics, and the rather inept Spanish South American foreign policy, this scheme was doomed to failure. The 'incondicionales' were certain that they had much to fear from the Colossus of the North. They cordially hated the Monroe Doctrine and regarded Pan-Americanism with deep suspicion. Blaine's Pan-Americanism greatly intensified their fear as to the method that the United States would use in its conquest of Latin America. Did not Blaine try to form an American Zollverein? What, then, was this but economic penetration?

In the Latin mind the mercantile republic of the north was conducting its foreign policy in the best tradition of a successful and unscrupulous merchant. That republic had bought its way across the North American continent and had forcibly ejected those who would not be bought. This new Carthaginian nation had tried to buy the "ever faithful" island, that Pearl of the Antilles. It was extending its influence in the Caribbean and in Latin America by means of business, which would soon demand the aid of the army

---

* Two supporters of the federal constitution were Nicolás Salmerón and Francisco Pi y Margall. The most outstanding of the unitarians was Emilio Castelar.

** Hans Kohn explains Pan-Hispanism in the Encyclopedia of the Social Sciences, Vol. XI. The following is paraphrased. Pan-Hispanism is a movement to create a general rapprochement based on tradition and sentiment; to cultivate between the Spanish speaking peoples of the world a relationship of cultural reciprocity and mutual sympathy. Although the origins of Pan-Hispanism may be traced back into the nineteenth century, it first began to gather force immediately after the withdrawal of Spain from effective political influence in the western hemisphere, that is, after the Spanish-American War. At the same time that this desire of the Spanish-American nations for a cultural rapprochement with Spain manifested itself there was a reaction against the position of the U. S. in the New World. Some protagonists have urged a revival of Spanish political power in the western hemisphere by means of a return of the f rmer American colonies to the Mother Country. Others have urged closer co-operation in the pursuit of common political and economic interests. However, these movements have had little success. Of far greater importance are the visits of Spanish authors and academicians to South America; the exchange of literature; the efforts of Spanish Americans to revise the historiography of the colonial period and to puncture the 'leyenda negra' and in general to substitute Spain for France as the gateway to European culture.

and navy. It must be admitted that precedent gave the conservatives good reason to fear American foreign policy. The name of civilization had been invoked against the Indians, the Monroe Doctrine against monarchical Europe, and now Pan-Americanism was being used as a disguise for the Yankee sweep into Latin America. Consequently the American foreign policy was distrusted, and liberals were warned to take heed of history and to draw closer to the Mother Country.

(1) Boletín Mercantil, June 13, November 2, October 21, 1888; January 18, October 23, 27, November 22, 1889; March 18, April 19, 1891; February 19, March 20, April 6, 1892; January 20, February 19, March 1, May 28, June 4, August 11, October 18, 25, 1893; January 12, 19, June 3, December 9, 1894; August 25, November 3, 20, 27, 1895; September 27, 1896; January 30, 1898.
(2) Abril, Mariano: Sensaciones de un Cronista, p. 8.
(3) Revista Mercantil, September 13, 1895.
(4) El País, December 26, 1896.
(5) El País, July 21, 1896.
(6) La Correspondencia de Puerto Rico, January 9, 1897.
(7) Boletín Mercantil, June 21, 1897.
(8) El País, January 3, 1896.
El Buscapié, January 31, February 28, 1892; January 18, 1894; April 10, 1896.
El Clamor del País, June 30, 1892.
(9) Boletín Mercantil, March 30, 1890; June 28, 1891; January 3, 1892; July 25, 1897.
El Buscapié, May 7, 1896.
El Clamor del País, March 1, 1888.
(10) La Correspondencia de Puerto Rico, March 9, 1897.
(11) La Democracia, November 13, 1897.
(12) El País, December 29, 1896.
(13) Boletín Mercantil, April 22, 1888; February 21, 1890; January 29, 1892; July 20, 1894; September 20, 1896; February 20, 1898.
(14) Boletín Mercantil, November 22, 1891; March 29, 1896; June 21, 1897.
El Buscapié, June 4, December 21, 1896.
La Correspondencia de Puerto Rico, August 9, October 25, 1897.

The Economic Factor

Part I: Minor Crops

The economic relations between the Antilles and the United States have always been important, due to the complementary character of the products of the two regions. Puerto Rico has always been in a position to supply a good part of the tropical products such as sugar, tobacco, and coffee which the United States needed. Of course, the larger Antille, Cuba, has always enjoyed the advantages of its closer location, its more fertile soil, and its larger area. Puerto Rico, nevertheless, played an important part in the commercial relations between the United States and the Antilles.

Puerto Rico was not a self-sufficient island during the nineteenth century. Its single crop economy forced it to import most of its food from abroad, principally from the United States. When the suppliers of certain foods could not fulfill their contracts owing to rains, revolutions, or drouth, the United States was regarded as the only possible source. When a revolution broke out in San Salvador it became impossible for the bean growers to live up to their contract. Consequently, the paper stated that the beans, so necessary to the poor, would have to be imported from the North.[1]

The economic dependence of Puerto Rico on the United States was further emphasized by articles dealing with the sale of coffee and tobacco in the North.[2] Home industries were advocated in order to decrease that inferior relationship between the island and the mainland.[3]

Puerto Rico needed the American market primarily. Another reason for its dependence upon the commercial goodwill of the United States was that, because of its dense population within a small area and dependence on sugar as its most profitable money crop, Puerto Rico needed the food products of the North. Spain was far away, had a relatively small population in comparison with the United States, and was unable to absorb the great quantities of sugar and tobacco produced by Puerto Rico. The obvious remedy for the economic situation was to develop the commercial relations between Puerto Rico and the Northern Republic.

However, there were many obstacles which had to be overcome before Puerto Rico could realize her commercial ambition. Those obstacles were American tariffs, Spanish laws which restricted trade unnecessarily, and the natural fear of Spanish authorities that closer economic relations between the United States and Puerto Rico would weaken the political bonds between the island and the Mother Country. The patriotic element, thus was introduced by the 'incondicionales' of Puerto Rico into the already difficult economic situation. They wanted no arrangement between the United States and Spain which might lessen the conservative hold on Puerto Rico. They feared that an increased commerce between the Northern Republic and the Antilles would ultimately turn Puerto Ricans to dangerous thinking. That thinking which might lead to autonomy, independence, or annexation was to be prevented at all costs. Between a better economic condition for Puerto Rico which might weaken the conservative grasp on the island and a feudal barter system which meant a static economic situation, the conservatives chose the latter. It was a selfish attitude but one to be justified on grounds of patriotism and loyalty to the Mother Country.

Desire to improve economic relations between the United States and Puerto Rico promoted articles on practically every subject ranging from steamship connections to the naturally important products of sugar, tobacco, and coffee. Even the Boletín Mercantil praised the establishment of a new marine service between New York and Puerto Rico on the grounds that anything which increased the facilities of commerce for Puerto Rico was to be encouraged.[4] The lack of a regular steamship service between Puerto Rico and Spain was deplored. It was felt that if every European country could have a regular passenger and mail service to the United States, Spain could at least do that much for its colony, Puerto Rico. The island, the paper said, was completely isolated from Spain for twenty days out of each month due to the irregularity of the boat service. Let the authorities do something to improve that situation or else the Yankees would turn it to their own ends.[5]

The monetary system, whereby the Puerto Rican peso was quoted at a lower figure than the Mexican peso was a handicap as great as the lack of transportation facilities. The reason given by the press for that situation was Spain's great distance from the province, which prevented her from knowing the problems of the island intimately.[6] The exchange, therefore, was so high as to paralyze business operations with the United States. This was illustrated by the fact that English ships which formerly stopped at Puerto Rico no longer did so, for lack of cargo. There were many complaints relative to that situation and to the bad economic condition of the island, but the Madrid government, seemingly, ignored them. El País remarked bitterly that the Eco Nacional of Madrid pretended to know more about the Puerto Rican situation than the Puerto Ricans themselves and gave misleading advice to the government.[7]

La Correspondencia de Puerto Rico co-öperated in the campaign to advertise Puerto Rican coffee in the United States and to create a market there. One such article lectured Puerto Ricans on American coffee-drinking habits. The Yankees, the paper said, did not drink coffee like the Puerto Ricans. The North Americans took a big cup of coffee, a half pint size, three times daily with their meals. They did not wait until the dinner was finished to take their coffee. On the contrary, they took a drink of coffee with every mouthful of food in order to save time. The lesson to be derived from this illustration, continued the paper, was to teach the North Americans to drink the concentrated coffee of Puerto Rico which would serve two laudable purposes. It would save the Americans the time that they considered so valuable and it would double the consumption of Puerto Rican coffee in the United States.[8]

It was reported that the landladies of the Yankee boarding-houses made their coffee each Monday from a mixture of corn, flour, and bad coffee, which concoction was to last for the rest of the week. A correspondent of the paper related that it had been his misfortune to drink that kind of coffee during the five years that he was a student in the United States. When he saw his fellow American students drinking that unsavory brew he came to the conclusion that there was some real anatomical difference between the Yankees and Puerto Ricans in their sense of taste. He had had an experience in connection with a store's campaign to make the public Moca-coffee-conscious. A sales-lady asked him if he would like to taste a cup of the best coffee in the world and then gave him a cup of the advertised coffee. The liquid to him was little better than water. He then speculated on the reasons why the coffee of Venezuela, Nicaragua, Haiti and "all the other trifling republics in America" were well known in the United States while that of Puerto Rico was unknown. During one of his conversations with his American friends upon the subject of coffee he was asked if Puerto Rico was near to the Philippines. Because of incidents like that he felt the following sign should be placed in all American cafés, "Puerto Rico is a Spanish colony near to Santo Domingo in the Caribbean Sea; it has a population of about one million, a surplus in the budget, and the best coffee in the world."[9]

El Eco, a paper from the coffee town of Yauco, said that it did not know why so little Puerto Rican coffee was sold in the United States. The United States bought and consumed a great deal of coffee, its customs duties were low on that product, and it paid good prices, but Puerto Rico continued to send the bulk of its coffee to Europe. The paper reasoned that if prices were higher in Europe, the expenses of the transaction were in turn four or five times higher. The prices quoted by coffee buying firms in the United States were considered to be fair but, El Eco believed, they would rise when the quality of Puerto Rican coffee were once known to the Americans.[10]

La Correspondencia de Puerto Rico remarked that the rest of the world, with the exception of the United States, was converted to the superiority of Puerto Rican coffee. It seemed as though it were only necessary to convert the United States, which somehow had remained unreconstructed and oblivious to the merits of Puerto Rican coffee. As soon as that happened, continued the paper, the coffee problem of Puerto Rico would be solved to the great benefit of the coffee-growers and the island as a whole.[11]

All papers joined in the promotion of an agency whose purpose would be to make Puerto Rican coffee known in the United States. The press of the island took the credit for initiating the idea and did its best to win the co-öperation of the coffee-growers of Puerto Rico. Everyone seemed to desire the American market, but few people, other than the editors, did anything to propagandize for insular coffee.[12]

Ermelindo Salazar, a prominent coffee farmer, expressed his views on the coffee problem. One point that he made was that the excellent coffee of Puerto Rico was unknown in the United States as was proven by mercantile statistics; this condition was, in his opinion, an opportunity for Puerto Rico. He believed that it was time the American people should do away with the inferior coffee that they had been in the habit of drinking in such enormous quantities and buy Puerto Rican coffee. In order to achieve that end, he advised that Spain should do something to make Puerto Rican coffee known in the United States in order to stimulate its purchase. Therefore, in any revision of the treaty, that should be an integral part. Salazar believed that when the United States was convinced of the superior quality of the Puerto Rican coffee in comparison with that of Brazil, the United States would not hesitate to pay more for the Puerto Rican product and would abandon the cheaper and inferior Brazilian coffee.[13]

Tobacco was another product which the Puerto Rican press tried to promote in the United States. El País printed an article from the Reforma Agrícola which tried to prove that the United States was the natural market for Cuban tobacco. If that were true, the paper argued, Puerto Rico should also be considered because everyone knew that Puerto Rican tobacco was far superior to the Cuban product.[14] This argument was supported by the fact that Puerto Rico had been in the habit of exporting large quantities of tobacco to Cuba in the past. Now, Cuba had decided to grow her own tobacco, a decision which cut off an important market for the lesser Antille. The United States, the paper continued, was a country that bought much tobacco; therefore the Puerto Rican tobacco-growers should come to terms with the American importers.[15] The development of the American market, it was felt, would double the price of tobacco, stimulate the founding of new plantations, and improve the economic condition of the tobacco industry in Puerto Rico.[16]

Every industry in Puerto Rico, sugar,[17] platanos,[18] pineapples,[19] did its best to develop the American market. It was realized that the geographic position of Puerto Rico made the United States the natural market and that closer economic relations should be promoted.

All the Puerto Rican papers were united in their desire to improve economic conditions in Puerto Rico, but they disagreed as to the method. Conservatives looked to Spain, liberals looked to the United States. La Balanza estimated that there were from eight to ten million Spaniards in the Peninsula who smoked at least two cigars daily, or a total of twenty million cigars smoked without the help of the Yankees. It declared the same thing applied to sugar because it calculated Spain, in case of an emergency, could consume all the Puerto Rican crop. The result, in its opinion, would be a true reciprocity with the Peninsula and with Europe, leaving the United States with all its products on hand without buyers.[20]

The editor of La Razón considered his "distinguished colleague" a dreamer rather than an economist because if so many cigars could be smoked in Spain and so many pounds of sugar consumed there, why had that fact not been noticed before? The real point, in his opinion, was that while the United States loosened its trade restrictions, Spain tightened hers. He warned that unless La Balanza and the other conservative organs paid some attention to the true facts of the case, Puerto Rico would be ruined.[21]

Part II: King Sugar

The McKinley Bill was interpreted by the liberals as an opportunity to improve relations with the United States and to make a commercial treaty which would greatly benefit the island. Spain, according to the liberals, had followed a fatal policy in regard to Cuba and Puerto Rico. The Cuban debt was devouring the resources and energies of the greater Antille. The Cubans wanted their public debt to be merged with the public debt of Spain because most of the obligation had been incurred during the Ten Years' War. The Mexican War and the intervention in Santo Domingo had also helped to burden Cuba with a debt that she was unable to pay. Instead of merging the Cuban debt with the Spanish, the Mother Country had imposed export, transit, and consumption taxes upon the island. Similar taxes were in operation in Puerto Rico.[22]

Those taxes, together with the Spanish monopolies in the islands, did much to support the arguments of the liberals. They argued that if Spain closed the door to the free entry of Cuban and Puerto Rican products into Spain, by virtue of what principle of equity and justice Spanish products were to be permitted free entry into the A..tilles? Why should Spanish products enjoy a privilege that those of the Antilles did not have? Perhaps that could be explained on the basis of patriotism was the sarcastic comment of the liberal press. Perhaps Spain wanted to exact from the Antilles as a show of patriotism, suicide on the altar of the Mother Country in order not to incur the epithet of 'traidor'![23]

La Razón asked what Las Novedades expected the Antilles to do when the United States closed her ports to the Cuban and Puerto Rican products.

Did that paper expect the Antilleans to cross their arms and to let themselves be carried away by patriotic idylls while the islands were going to ruin? It was pointed out that some Puerto Rican papers (a direct reference to the Boletín Mercantil) thought they had found a remedy for the danger in a patriotic theory. Those Quixotes and idealists believed that Spain would consume all the Puerto Rican sugar and tobacco in order to prove to McKinley that true patriots still existed in the world. La Razón was of the opinion that McKinley did not care one way or the other whether there were true patriots in Spain or not. Las Novedades said that the people of the Antilles had given to Spain so great proofs of patriotism and had made so many sacrifices on the altar of nationality that it could not doubt the sincerity of Antillean desires.[24]

That seemed to the liberals rather belated recognition. Unfortunately, they said, that famous patriotism had been abused so much and such great sacrifices had been exacted from the people of the Antilles in the name of that sacrosanct sentiment that it no longer received the old respect. Experience and disappointment had changed what was once a noble fanaticism into something that was now subordinated to reason and logic.[25]

The time limit set by the McKinley Bill was accepted as a normal procedure, but forward-looking men were disturbed by the procrastinating policy of the Spanish authorities. Studies upon any matter were interminable in Madrid. Therefore, the liberals protested that declarations to the effect that the home government was doing its best to restore happiness to the Puerto Rican people were useless in this hour of crisis. The necessity was to formulate closer relations with the United States and to forget pious confidence in Divine Providence and in the grandeur of the Spanish cause.

The learned men of Madrid informed Puerto Rico that they had the real key for the situation in their discovery that the bill represented the true political attitude of Blaine.* That announcement did little to calm the restless liberals who cared little about the true attitude of Blaine, or anyone else for that matter. They wanted immediate action free from any speculation regarding the motives behind the bill. The Spanish governmental leaders were compared with the persons referred to in the Bible who "having eyes yet are blind, ears yet are deaf."

Common sense counted for nothing with the government, opined the liberals, if one were to judge by their actions. Studies were promised on the economic relations between Puerto Rico and the United States, but, according to La Razón, based on the false assumption that the issue was predominately political. First of all, there was the discovery that Blaine's political views motivated the bill; secondly, there were those who pretended to see in the bill evidences of the Monroe Doctrine and imperialism. What, asked the paper, did the McKinley Bill and the new Yankee tariffs have to do with the Monroe Doctrine?[26] The paper repeated that the authorities should not regard the United States as imperialistic and concerned for its own welfare. However, the latter point was natural, said the editor. The Americans must take care of their own interests; no one else would. It was a question of dollars and pesos and should be solved in those terms; nothing would be gained by arguing that the Yankee policy was one of "America for the Americans".[27]

---

* The conservatives felt that American tariff policy toward the Caribbean countries had but one purpose: economic penetration to be followed by political domination.

The North Americans, before anything else, were practical economists. They looked to profits from business rather than to the dubious gains from a colonial empire. They preferred commercial dependencies to territorial annexations. The paper remarked that anyone who knew any geography at all would easily understand that although the Yankees accepted the Monroe Doctrine as an integral part of their political beliefs, business and business alone motivated their present policy. The geographical consideration which the paper referred to was the still unexploited Great American West that was relatively uninhabited. Consequently, the paper pointed out, it would be unpolitic for the United States to embark upon any imperialistic program such as the conservatives feared could result from the McKinley Bill.[28]

Further news upon the McKinley Bill prompted the liberal press to agitate for a closer economic union with the United States. The proposition of reciprocity in regard to sugar was termed the salvation of Puerto Rico since the United States was the island's only large scale consumer of sugar.[29] The opposition to the said reciprocity came from the 'incondicionales' who promoted fantastic theories---economic, financial, administrative---and some which were supposedly patriotic. All of them tended to depreciate the importance of the Yankee proposition, and to create a fairy-land of free coastal trade, and invariably ending their arguments by asking "What in the ---- do we want the American market for anyway?"

That kind of an argument was considered a mania and an obsession by the liberal press who felt that the conservatives were so blinded by their hatred of the United States that they forgot the needs of Puerto Rico. The liberals advised their opponents to consider the situation realistically and to forget any antipathy they might have toward the Union. The needs of the island should transcend personal feelings in their opinion. There were many motives, the press felt, why Spain should accept the American version of reciprocity and thus draw closer economic bonds between Puerto Rico and the United States.

The first reason was a very simple one, "Either we sell our sugar or we do not"; if the latter happened, Puerto Rico would be bankrupt and an ennumeration of the other motives would be a waste of time. A Cuban writer asked a hypothetical question of the Minister of Ultramar, "How much of the Cuban sugar is consumed by Spain?" It was estimated that Spain used perhaps three hundred thousand tons, which still left four hundred thousand tons of unsalable sugar. The hypothetical conversation continued. "Would England buy any? No, she has colonies to supply her needs. Will France? Less. Germany? ---Even less. Italy? Do not even think about her."[30]

It was shown to the satisfaction of the liberals that unless closer economic relations with the United States were formed there would be no one either in Europe or America to buy Antillean sugar. Since that condition was true, the liberals wondered if the central government wanted the Antilles to go a little more bankrupt than they already were.[31] Possible ruin, they felt, was the contingency which the politicians and Chambers of Commerce ignored, much to the detriment of the farmers and merchants. On the contrary, they talked about coastal trade with Spain as being a remedy for the situation when Puerto Rican products could no longer be exported to the United States. The paper countered by stating that little Puerto Rican tobacco was smoked and little Puerto Rican coffee drunk in the Metropoli. La Razón did not agree with its conservative colleague, La Balanza, which felt that simply by virtue of a royal order seventeen million Spaniards would suddenly turn to Antillean products and thus obviate the necessity of the American market.[32]

Every economic action of the American Congress that had the slight-
est relation to Puerto Rico received much space in the Puerto Rican press
and was commented on in many ways. The conservative press invariably
interpreted the action as one which would further the American economic
penetration and future political domination of the Antilles. Fear, suspicion,
and even hatred characterized the conservative reception of new American
economic legislation.[33]

It was deemed difficult to deal with the United States upon a basis of
equitable reciprocity because American commercial treaties were considered unilateral in the sense that they represented an American effort to
create a customs union advantageous to the United States but hard for the
Spanish-American peoples. Articles as lard and codfish paid little duty
when they entered Puerto Rico. Those were food products and articles of
first necessity and had to be within easy reach of the people. On the other
hand, it was pointed out, sugar imported into the United States paid a large
duty which did much to increase the economic distress of Puerto Rico. Sugar also was an article of first necessity to the Puerto Rican people. When
sugar was high and the American tariff low, the island prospered greatly;
when the duty was high and prices low, the economic effect on the island was
as disastrous as a hurricane.[34]

Even the conservative papers condemned legislative hindrances for-
mulated by Spain in answer to American tariff reductions. At one time the
Committee of Ways and Means of the American Congress recommended a
reduction in the sugar duties. It was believed that this recommendation
would soon be law; all joined in predicting that Cuba and Puerto Rico would
be greatly benefited because of their proximity to the American market.
The Cuban reaction to the proposal was quoted at length in the Puerto Rican
papers and their satisfaction with the proposed law was noted. However,
the Cortes passed a measure that increased the export tax on Cuban sugar,
thus eliminating any possible benefit of the American reduction. That action,
to the press, was a blunder and one which should not be repeated in respect
to Puerto Rico. Why, it was asked, should the Spanish legislators work not
only to neutralize the effect of the American concession but also to create
greater difficulties for the exportation of Antillean sugars and to close the
only natural market open to that sugar?[35]

The McKinley Tariff of 1890 seemed to fulfill all the prophesies of the
conservatives concerning the Colossus of the North. That tariff gave the
United States a weapon to hold over South American countries. Certain articles commonly imported from Latin America such as molasses, coffee,
and hides were placed on the free list, with the proviso that the President
might impose duties on them in case of any nation which levied "unjust or
unreasonable" duties on American products.[36] Consequently Puerto Rico
was greatly affected by the new tariff. If Spain refused to make a commercial treaty with the United States which would permit the favorable entry of
American farm and industrial products into the Spanish Antilles, Spain would
be judged as following an "unjust or unreasonable" policy toward the United
States. The tariff would then be enforced to the letter and the United States
would get its sugar, tobacco, and coffee from some other country. Cuba and
Puerto Rico would enter into an economic decline and Spain would be to
blame for not making a treaty with the United States. Nevertheless, the
treaty was made, but it and the McKinley tariff were denounced vehemently
in many of the Puerto Rican papers. Both were felt to be unjust and disadvantageous to Puerto Rico.

The North American people were felt to have an expansive spirit

similar to that of the Carthaginians, their only desire being to convert all
the peoples of the Americas into mercantile colonies for exploitation by the
United States. That was proved to the satisfaction of the conservative editors by the fiasco of the Pan-American Congress of 1888-1889 and by the
McKinley Tariff. The United States was accused of wanting to form the two
continents into only one great republic or empire. Those tendencies, according to the conservatives, had been apparent ever since the time of Monroe
when (according to the conservative papers) he coined that famous phrase
"America for the Americans." This phrase, now, was translated to mean
"America for the North Americans or the Yankees".[37]

Blaine, in their opinion, revealed that phrase in its true light. He had
proposed a confederation of the two Americas by means of treaties and mercantile relations which, in the long run, would have very little advantages
for the Latin-American republics. The paper believed that McKinley was
following the same policy as Blaine but with greater acumen. The customs
tariffs proposed by McKinley, in the opinion of the Boletin, constituted a
real economic revolution for many countries and an attack upon international
good-will. The goal of that tariff was to stop the importation of articles
which could compete with American industry. It was highly protectionist
and was correspondingly condemned by foreign nations.[38]

Spain was one of the foreign nations that had to comply with the terms
of the McKinley Tariff because of her position as an American power. She
could not absorb the products of the Antilles alone; the United States' market was a necessity. The Puerto Rican conservative press remarked that
such a procedure was strange at a time when the policy of nations was to
establish reciprocal trade agreements. However, it was admitted that one
benefit of the tariff was that it provided for the free importation of raw sugar into the United States. But that advantage was more apparent than real
because, the conservative press continued, the American government gave
two cents per pound bounty to the domestic producers of cane and beet sugar. The alternative which was suggested was that Spain should make a definite commercial treaty with the United States relative to the main products
of Puerto Rico: sugar, tobacco, and coffee. The American government had
gone violently from one extreme to the other, in the opinion of the paper. It
warned the United States that its treasury might have a surplus but that surplus's could not last forever. Rome, it cautioned, had fallen because of its
own weight and grandeur. Let the United States take notice![39]

The McKinley Tariff was productive of much moralizing and of much
printing of foreign comment on the part of the liberal papers. Protests
against this bill, they said, came from all parts of the world. It was remarked that when people lived in groups they must regard the rights of
others. The implication was that the United States had disregarded that
duty by passing such a tariff. It was predicted that the tariff would cause
trouble not only to Puerto Rico but also for American business enterprises.
Protectionism was a weapon forged in the United States and thrown at the
other nations; but, La Razón warned, it could rebound and hurt the United
States. The English press said that the tariff, by closing the American ports
to European goods, would open the ports of England to world commerce, to
the detriment of the United States.[40]

Ill effects were envisaged for the Chicago Exposition, because it was
alleged that foreign countries would not pay such high customs duties just to
display those products which were discriminated against. Italy had already
dissolved its World's Fair committee. France remarked that the tariff was
an ingratitude on the part of the Yankees to Europe, who had populated and

strengthened America by Old World immigrants. The <u>London Times</u> considered the bill hostile to England. An American correspondent in Berlin said that the German government would make reprisals if the Yankees did not modify the tariff. The paper pointed out that the bill was already causing trouble in the United States because prices were rising so fast as to cause a real crisis. It was asked what effect the bill would have upon Spain. The answer was that it was too early (1890) as yet to make any predictions but one thing was felt to be self-evident: the United States had forgotten that in matters of public interest there were many duties which had to be taken into consideration. The Yankee nation erected a temple to protectionism, forgetting that free commerce must be the basic principle of any country which was really free and democratic.[41]

To many Puerto Ricans it appeared as though the United States was trying to defy the world by its commercial policy, which had been condemned by all the foreign nations and even by many Americans. Many European industries had been forced to dismiss their workers and to close their shops. Those bankrupt industries and unemployed workers demanded that some reprisal be made against the United States. The American tariff was considered a great bar between foreign nations and the Union. Gladstone said the McKinley Tariff was a great mistake and many innocent people would suffer. The <u>Boletín</u> advised the Mother Country to import her cotton, wheat, oil, and flour from some nation other than the United States in order to lessen the danger of that 'sword of Damocles' (the McKinley Tariff). It was hoped that the commotion raised in Europe would open the eyes of the Yankees and that a new law would be passed to repair the fatal consequences of the hated tariff.[42]

One liberal paper wondered just what the Mother Country was doing to alleviate the effects of the new tariff. It noted that the McKinley Bill was already 'under study' by the home government but little was expected from that action. For anything to be 'under study' by the central government meant that a conclusion would be reached some time in the distant future. Meanwhile, the paper continued, Puerto Rico and her people faced a black and hopeless future if the actions of the government were to be taken as a guide.[43]

Foreign ships raced to arrive in the United States before the new tariff went into operation. There were many accounts of ships that got in under the line and consequently did not have to pay the new duty. When such incidents happened the jubilation of the importers and the captains was described at length. The New York City Customs House was reported to be working over-time due to the sudden rush of ships to that city.[44]

It was noted that due to the McKinley Bill much had been said in Europe about a system of economic reprisals against the United States. A French paper examined the whole question from the French point of view and proved that that nation could not afford to adopt such a plan because she was the one that had the least complaint against the bill. It appeared that the tariff had been aimed against Canada and Germany, which exported great quantities of industrial and agricultural products to the United States. The Americans, in the opinion of the paper, came to the conclusion that such importations were harmful to infant industries and had passed the new tariff to save themselves. The French, then, did not favor the European economic coalition. France felt that if she entered into the combination, she would merely be pulling the German and English chestnuts out of the fire to the detriment of French commerce. The French paper went on to remark that all products coming from the United States were already heavily taxed.

Those products were articles of first necessity, and France could never carry on a tariff war against the United States because of the French dependence on American wheat, oil, cotton, etc. However, as far as Cuba and Puerto Rico were concerned, there was no way except reciprocity; without it would come economic ruin.[45]

It was felt that the general public ought to know that the provisions of that famous tariff had been universally considered as a declaration of war upon the commercial world. The provisions of the bill were given in detail, and the obvious conclusion was that Spain should make a treaty with the United States in spite of the advantages which the United States would receive. It was pointed out that Spain had no choice in the matter if she wanted to save the interests of her colonies in the Antilles. If the date fixed by the American government came without Spain's having taken any action to make a commercial treaty, a crisis would result in Puerto Rico and Cuba. The sugar, coffee, and tobacco of the two Antilles would remain in those islands, to the financial ruin of the producers.

La Razón predicted the course that the 'true patriots' would follow. That course, it prophesied, would be one of trying to increase the free coastal trade between Puerto Rico and the Metropoli in order to establish stronger political relations between the two places. That, in the opinion of the paper, was a mistake because those patriots followed the erroneous policy of interpreting the present situation in political terms, whereas the only solution was economic. It was felt that no matter how great a show of patriotism was made, Puerto Rico would not obtain any advantage because Spain could not compete with the United States in matters of money, consumption, or industries. Her market was insufficient for the needs of the Antilles. The paper said that those facts were known by everyone except the Puerto Rican Utopians, who made fantastic figures without consulting logic or statistics. It was pointed out that if the independent countries of South America anticipated Spain and made commercial treaties with the United States on the basis of the McKinley Tariff, they would gain all that Cuba and Puerto Rico were losing. The Antilles, then, would not be in a position to pay even the reduced expenses of government. Rather than have that situation, the paper advised the government to make an end of interminable studies because the interests of the Antilles demanded a speedy solution of the problem.[46]

El Globo of Madrid was quoted at length in the Puerto Rican press in spite of the divergence of opinion between the insular and Spanish press concerning the purpose of the McKinley Bill. The Spanish paper tried to calm those who believed that the McKinley Bill would inevitably ruin the Cuban and Puerto Rican production. It said that the system that the government of the United States had followed since the Republicans came to power was of profound political interest although it appeared to be of purely commercial nature. It felt that this bill really confirmed the policy begun by Blaine in the Pan-American movement. The Yankees were alleged to have studied the matter well before converting it into a law. El Globo thought that the McKinley Bill was more theatrical than positive although, it was admitted, there were some teeth in the bill. To the paper it appeared at first sight that the United States wanted to close its ports to the products of Europe, but the true purpose of the bill in the eyes of El Globo, was political because the United States looked forward to the day when there would be no European country with colonies in the New World. The North American nation wanted to be supreme from Canada to Tierra del Fuego. The only countries felt to be able to make any resistance to the United States were Argentina and Brazil, but they were considered as being far from able to measure their strength with the Colossus of the North. It was predicted that by the time that they had the population, industries, and navies similar to the Union, the prosperity of the United States would be even greater.[47]

The United States knew, then, that its superiority of population, riches, and territory made the European colonies in the New World dependent on the maintenance of mercantile relations with the western republic. The only condition on which the United States would open its markets to Europe, according to El Globo, would be that of an American freedom of action with the European colonies. Those colonies were industrially poor;---the United States, rich. Therefore, the paper continued, the Yankees would become de facto owners of those territories. The only way for the European nations to fight the industrial weapon of the United States was for those nations to establish great industries in their American colonies. It was predicted that if Cuba did not develop industrially with the same rapidity as Belgium, at the end of fifty years, Cuba would be a financial vassal of the United States. At the end of that time, then, Cuba (and Puerto Rico) would be a New World Portugal, a rather prosperous nation but one lacking all commercial and economic independence. Therefore, in the opinion of the paper, the only thing for the European nations to do was to make each and every one of the Antilles into prosperous industrial centers. Spain, it urged, should follow its historical tradition as an imperial nation.[48]

The liberal papers disagreed with their Spanish colleague as to the possible success of industries in the Antilles in competition with the United States. They declared that they had heard about that possibility for the past ten years and not one industry had been established in the Antilles by 1890. They did not want to deny that those sugar refineries might be established. If such an enterprise were founded by Spain, then Puerto Rico, they said would soon deposit in Spain all the sugar that the Peninsula wanted. But granting such a miracle, they still wanted to know just what Spain was going to do about Antillean tobacco. If those questions were answered satisfactorily, the liberals would worry no more about the McKinley Bill. The liberals wanted it understood that, while they insisted that the Mother Country make a treaty of reciprocity with the United States to take care of the sugar crop and thus save the island from ruin, the request did not mean that Spain should turn the Antilles over to Mr. Blaine to dispose of at his discretion; nor did they demand that the Peninsular interests should suffer.[49]

El Globo was convinced that there were neither annexionists nor separatists in either Cuba or Puerto Rico, because the Spaniards in those islands realized that absorption by the United States would be a great humiliation. In order that the people of those Antilles should be drawn closer to Spain the paper recommended that the customs and electoral reform be tackled at once. The first, so that the colonial budgets would not lack funds and the products lack markets; the latter, so that the Cortes would receive a better and more just representation from the American provinces. Everyone, it was said, agreed to the necessity of those reforms. After those reforms were law, then the government could follow commercial policies inspired only by Spanish commercial interests. In that way, concluded the article, would Spain avoid being dependent upon European nations in matters of colonial policy.[50]

The editor of La Razón disagreed with the apprehensions and predictions of El Globo. The stand of the Puerto Rican paper was that the background of the McKinley Bill was economic and not political. It justified its deduction on the ground that the Yankees were practical men, men of numbers. That expression meant that the Americans were financially minded

and never risked anything in adventures, especially if those adventures
seemed to be of an impulsive and an impractical nature. It was said that
the Yankees did not favor annexations that would disturb their peace and
prosperity. According to the paper, Americans as a whole believed that
the Monroe Doctrine would be applied when the moment arrived for its application and nothing would be done to disturb the political status quo. In
the opinion of the paper the object of the McKinley Bill was no other, as far
as the United States was concerned, than to monopolize the greatest possible number of business enterprises in the Western World.[51]

Two papers, one liberal and one conservative, tried to explain to
their readers the reasons why the United States had adopted a tariff which
apparently did nothing other than to antagonize foreign nations. The reason
for their action was not that they were particularly pro-American but that
they desired to clarify the situation and to prevent the political atmosphere
from becoming too emotional. The papers announced that the great question
of trading was still on the floor of the American Congress and if the South
American countries wished to gain advantages that now would be the time
to act. American policy, they said, was not determined by theoretical but
by realistic and eminently practical considerations. If the United States decided to permit the free importation of sugar into the Union it did so for a
specific reason which could be explained in terms of business. That nation
was not going to voluntarily give up a portion of its revenue (customs duties)
and receive nothing in return.

The idea held by many people that the United States should open up its
markets to the products of the Americas without those countries making reciprocal concessions was ridiculous in the opinion of those papers. It was
true that there was a surplus in the Federal Treasury but that did not prevent the Americans from being businesslike in their commercial dealings
with foreign nations. The liberal paper stated that it was purely a question
of "Give me this and I will give you that" applied to international trade relations. The solution of the problem was a matter of urgent necessity for
Puerto Rico and it was felt that the Spanish government should be grateful
for so rich a nation as the United States giving attention to a matter which
would favor the other nations of America. Trade currents, said the paper,
coursed by way of reciprocity---advantages to be given according to com-
pensations received which was a just way of doing.[52]

Blaine's views were quoted relative to reciprocity. He felt that rich
countries should not expect complete reciprocity from poorer countries but
that anything received from them was a gain. Wherever the United States
made a concession it should receive something in return because no nation
ever made treaties without deriving some practical benefit. He did not accept the argument that a treaty made with one nation should necessarily be
repeated with all nations because that would destroy the reason motivating
such a treaty. Some nations, due to the nature of their needs, naturally fitted into reciprocity arrangements better than others. As a result, he believed, reciprocity was circumstantial and such treaties could not be applied
to all nations alike.

Those were Blaine's ideas and the press speculated on the future of
Puerto Rico. The Puerto Rican papers felt that the Deputies representing
Puerto Rico at the Cortes should take advantage of the time limit stipulated
in the McKinley Bill before it was too late. The duty of the press, as seen
by the editors, was to immediately arouse the Deputies and the people of
Puerto Rico from their inertia.[53]

News circulated in Puerto Rico that sugar would enter the United States free of duty which caused an immediate rise of optimism among the Puerto Rican agriculturists. La Razón tried to restrain the overly ebullient spirits by warning that the United States was not thinking of granting that advantage to Puerto Rican sugar free. It felt that the United States was considering reciprocity methods in order to equalize that pretended free gift. The idea behind the arrangement, it felt, was to emphasize a policy of free markets with the Americans in order to be able to control the commerce which the Americans had with Europe. The editors, in general, repeated their previous warning that the United States was not entering any commercial agreement purely for the sake of South America. The thing was clear to the press. It felt the Yankees knew that their markets were the natural markets for the Spanish-American countries and were making the most of that situation. Cuba, for example, in 1889 exported to the United States fifty-two million pesos worth of products and imported only eleven millions from the North.[54] The vital fact, the press insisted, was that the United States imported from the Antilles that huge amount of goods in exchange for the relatively few things which Cuba and Puerto Rico imported from the United States.[55] Such a situation, in the opinion of La Razón, was one which the practical Yankees would not continue indefinitely. The United States, therefore, would demand reciprocal concessions for its agricultural and manufactured products. "Do not be surprised when that situation develops" was the prophetic warning of the editor.[56]

The liberal Puerto Rican papers became quite bitter over the apparent indifference of the Spanish government and the local chambers of commerce to the problems of Puerto Rico. It has been mentioned that one of the liberal papers favored a realistic treatment of the economic situation threatened by the McKinley Bill. That paper became increasingly acid in its comments when it observed the pessimism in Puerto Rico concerning the economic future of the island. It emphasized that the editors of the paper were not farmers, merchants, manufacturers, nor ship-owners, and that therefore, the paper was defending no special interest. What the paper did condemn in no uncertain terms was the inertia of those in power who slept in the face of the island's crisis and unhappiness. The Chambers of Commerce of San Juan and Ponce, in the opinion of the paper, had done nothing to remedy the evils that necessarily would come to Puerto Rico the moment that the United States closed its ports to insular products. It advised that the best procedure was to follow Cuba in its efforts to spur the Spanish government to action. But, it mourned, the paper was preaching in a desert because no one seemed to have noticed that Puerto Rico was facing a grave and important matter, one that would not wait upon the inertia of either the Madrid government or the chambers of commerce.[57]

Cuba, the paper showed did not regard the economic situation with the same indifference as did the conservatives of Puerto Rico. There, even the conservatives recognized that the only salvation was some kind of an understanding with the United States and Cuba was determined to see that come to pass. The realization of that aim would mean, said the paper, that Cuba would have an abundance of everything and that Puerto Rico would have an abundance of its own products.[58]

La Razón remarked sarcastically, "Well, sir,... those devils of the Yankees work more in favor of Puerto Rico than all the Becerras, Fabié,*

---

* Manuel Becerra y Bermudez, 1823-1896, was a Spanish leader identified with the revolutionary republican cause. He worked actively for revolution in 1848, 1854, and 1868; Deputy to the Cortes, 1869; Minister of Ultramar, 1869, 1888.

and all the other lawyers ... of Spain." That comment was prompted by the observation that shortly before, the Yankees had almost solved the exchange of the Mexican silver for Spanish gold by maintaining the bi-metallic standard. The monetary problem, according to the paper, had been 'under study' in the Madrid archives for years without anything having been done about it. Now those 'incondicionales' who saw a broom as musket and every such musket as a threat to their governmental plum would immediately condemn the probable American demand for reciprocity! Those patriots, said the paper, would shout to high heaven and would insist that the reduced tariff on sugar was merely one more step toward grabbing the Antilles. However, the editor continued, Puerto Ricans should not forget that unless some agreement were made with the Yankees they would immediately increase the sugar duty and Puerto Rico would be unable to sell its sugar in the one and only natural market that it had. The only recourse, then, would be for the Puerto Ricans to eat their sugar because there would be no market. It was quite a problem and there were two ways of solving it. According to the paper, the government could through reciprocity either enrich the Puerto Rican farmers or could give them a stick and a bag and turn them into beggars. The editor had little doubt but that the latter method would finally be chosen by the authorities.[59]

According to a liberal paper, Puerto Rico had been juicy for the bureaucratic appetites because the island served as a means to elevate the inept Peninsular politicians who had failed in Spain and were now failing in Puerto Rico. Puerto Rico, it was felt, was being treated as though she were more foreign than any foreign country. The Madrid government, then, was doing nothing, but Cuba was taking action. Cánovas[*] asked all the commercial entities of the island to submit reports to inform the government about the economic problems of Puerto Rico and how they were affected by the new tariff law of the United States. That move on the part of the Spanish minister, in the opinion of La Razón, was completely useless and only adopted with the object of pretending that he was doing something about the situation. It was stated that the minister already had the resolutions passed by the Puerto Rican chambers of commerce. Were they not enough? Why, it was asked, waste any more time in resolutions and studies. The paper recommended that Spain should get together with the Yankees either through a commercial treaty or by a good reform in the tariff duties.[60]

One editor noted that Senator Aldrich[**] presented an amendment to the McKinley Bill authorizing the president to levy discriminatory taxes on those countries which did not accept the American principle of reciprocity. This was added fuel to the angry fire of the liberal press which demanded immediate action on the part of the Spanish government. It recognized the right of the United States to impose those prohibitory taxes. What it criticized was the fact that the Spanish government permitted such taxes to be imposed without acting in behalf of the Antilles. The United States, the lib-

---

Antonio Fabié y Escudero, 1834-1899, was a Spanish politician, writer, and lawyer; Deputy to the Cortes in 1863 and 1881; Minister of Ultramar in 1890; President of the Council of State, 1895-1897.

[*] Antonio Cánovas del Castillo, 1828-1897; Spanish statesman and author; Member of the Cortes, 1854; helped to draw up the Constitution of 1876 and reconstruct the Conservative Party at that time; Prime Minister four times; assassinated in 1897.

[**] Nelson Wilmarth Aldrich, 1841-1915; Member of Congress from Rhode Island, 1879-1881; U.S. Senator, 1881-1904; champion of Republican protectionism.

erals said, was the only natural market of Cuba and Puerto Rico and Spain should do something to save it. "Do something now before the Antilles have to join the beggars' union!" was the cry of the islands. However, it pleaded that the matter should not be submitted to the Minister of Ultramar because then Puerto Rican sugar would rot before anything was done. The 'studies' of the Minister of Ultramar were likened to those on yellow fever which had been 'studied' since Columbus discovered America with a report still due.[61]

The press observed that unless something were done soon, the high importation duties of the McKinley Bill would be imposed in January of 1892 on those countries that did not accept the American principle of commercial reciprocity. If those terms of the United States were not met by that time and Puerto Rico had to pay the high duties, Puerto Rico would not be able to compete successfully with those countries that accepted the American tariff proposal. Cánovas was felt to be too much involved with the Banco-boa, the ship-owners of Catalonia, the exploiters of the coastal trade, and the Spanish protectionists to do anything constructive about the Puerto Rican situation. The opinion of the press was that the Spanish government should transcend all political parties and vested interests in the face of the economic crisis.[62]

In comparison with the penetrating editorials of the liberal papers the arguments of the conservatives seem to be carping, vacillating, and weak. The McKinley Bill was referred to as "that infamous bill" and the "shield of protectionism". Those papers protested that they had met the McKinley Bill with logical statements, reinforced with their own judgment and experience, together with the defense of the European and American press. They waited for some one else to do something about the bill because they were certain the bill would not be maintained in face of the protests of the foreign countries and of the American people. Those countries that had commerce with the United States were not going to remain idle and do nothing about it![63]

Yet those very conservative papers offered little constructive criticism or remedies to save the island from the threatened crisis. McKinley's defeat in the Congressional elections, their own loyalty to Spain, and their attacks against the bill were all that the conservative papers could offer the island as panaceas.[64] Recrimination and the wisdom of hindsight were about the best that La Balanza offered in this controversy.[65]

The reply of the Boletín to attacks on the Chamber of Commerce was to make frequent references to "our active and efficient Chamber of Commerce", the study that it was making or about to make, and the many ways that the island had profited from its activities.[66] Those bodies, especially that of San Juan, were continually compiling statistics to prove one point or another---usually in support of the governmental attitude.

The commercial treaty with the United States which was finally ratified in the latter part of 1891, did not prove popular with the Spanish authorities. Therefore, the San Juan Chamber of Commerce published reports showing that the income of Puerto Rico had greatly diminished on account of the commercial treaty. The value of the American market to the Puerto Rican producers was admitted, but there were evils that followed that treaty which outweighed the advantages. Those evils, declared the report, were the decrease of the coastal trade with Spain, which had appeared so promising in 1890, a freight tax of ten per cent levied on all articles imported from Spain, and the importation of poor quality articles from the Mother Country. Those facts, in the opinion of the Chamber, produced the rare phenomenon that a foreign nation, the United States, was benefited at the expense of Spain. That body then suggested that there be no duties on articles imported from the Peninsula. It was felt that the central government failed to take into consideration the special circumstances of Puerto Rico (in comparison with Cuba) when there was any legislation touching the Antilles. That was the one main criticism which the Chamber offered concerning the Mother Country.[67]

The point made by the San Juan Chamber of Commerce that transit duties to and from Spain hindered the full development of Puerto Rican commerce was supported by Cuban papers. Those papers also agreed with La Razón that the McKinley Bill was the logical answer that the North American government could give to Spain relative to the customs duties imposed by the Mother Country on Antillean exports and imports. The Spanish government was accused of desiring to protect and to foster the commerce and industry of Spain at the expense of the foreigner and even of the Antilles. To foster home industry at the expense of the foreigner was understandable but to foster that industry at the expense of the provinces was not at all clear. It was stated that the Spanish government forgot that the United States consumed half of the tobacco and four-fifths of the sugar produced by the greater Antille.[68] The Puerto Rican exports of sugar to the United States was always more than half of the island's crop. However, there were only occasional shipments of tobacco and coffee to the United States.[69]

Great speculation as to the nature of the commercial treaty with the United States characterized political and journalistic circles in July of 1891. The rumors grew and multiplied so fast that the Royal Governor felt obliged to shed some light upon the situation. His information was of a general character, but two statements were of importance to the agriculture of the island. One touched the increased exportation of sugar to the United States, and the other concerned the future of the coastal trade between the Antilles and Spain.[70]

The Spanish government justified its new treaty on grounds of patriotism, of solicitude for the interests of the provinces, and of preference on the basis of nationality.[71] This was more or less to satisfy liberal attacks on the nature of the treaty. Those papers in Cuba had stated that unless some provision were made in the new treaty for Cuban sugar and tobacco Cuba would have to choose between two alternatives, economic death or annexation. The Boletín pointed out that there was no reason to be so pessimistic because the United States was not the only market in the world for Cuban sugar. Did not Europe consume sugar and tobacco? Cuba should go on and develop markets other than the United States for her products.[72] That was all very good advice and very easy to say but the facts remained that the bulk of the Cuban exports went to the United States and newspaper articles could not change it.

Economic conditions in Puerto Rico were unsettled in the latter part of 1891. Many reasons were given for the bad state of affairs but none of them offered any constructive criticism to right the situation. Masonry,[73] foreign economic interests,[74] and the McKinley Bill were all offered as factors to blame for the current depression. A provincial relief board met during 1891 under the presidency of the governor to consider the methods of solving the existing crisis. During the deliberations a scene took place reminiscent of a similar occurence during the French Revolution. In 1789, when the National Assembly was at its wits ends to know what to do about the financial situation, a very patriotic member of the middle class begged permission to address the Assembly. He did so for some two hours, telling

how the acute financial condition of France moved him greatly and how he
wanted to do his bit toward solving it. He then marched down to the president's stand and deposited his silver shoe buckles for the good of the treasury.

In 1891, a Mr. Rodríguez Fuentes, after doing much the same thing
before the governor and his council by explaining at length that the United
States in reality was to blame for the depression, then donated to the council "property valued at sixty pesos" for the betterment of the island. He
was thanked by the governor.[75] A writer who signed himself "X" believed
that the bad organization of the budget of the province of Puerto Rico was
partly to blame for the situation. He believed that it would be better for
the island if many of the overlapping governmental agencies were discon-
tinued and if the swarm of public officials were diminished. He did not approve of the destructive criticism made by so many of the newspaper
writers.[76]

The terms of the reciprocity treaty were published on August 16th,
1891. In the opinion of the Boletín it was a treaty made for the exclusive
benefit of the United States. That paper believed that the numerous concessions made in favor of the United States would result in the West Indies'
being reduced to a mere group of colonies of the United States or markets
for the American factories. It asked how the island was going to balance
its budget now that so many favors had been given to the United States and
also predicted that the Puerto Rican farmers would have a hard time. Many
small and large industries of the West Indies, it said, should resent the situation created by the pact and should protest. Protests had already been
made by the Catalan flour millers and industries, which, it believed, were
indicative of a general movement of discontent directed against the treaty.[77]

Catalan flour millers could protest as much as they pleased and bring
great pressure to bear on Madrid yet all this was unavailing. Home interests were always at a disadvantage when commercial treaties with the United States were concerned because of the geographic factor. No matter
what was said by the Spanish industries or the 'incondicionales' of Puerto
Rico, the location of the United States and the Puerto Rican need for American foodstuffs usually decided the argument in favor of the Colossus of the
North. Patriotism, love of country, and the past glories of Spain, then,
availed little against the McKinley Bill and the dependence of Puerto Rico
on the United States for food.

It was noted that the retailers of clothing and cotton goods had raised
their prices on account of a rise in Europe. However, the foodstuff merchants had not raised their prices because most of the food of Puerto Rico
came from the United States. This comparison taught an obvious lesson to
the readers---that it would be better for the Puerto Rican consumer if the
clothing merchants imported most of their goods from the United States
rather than the Old World.[78]

Great quantities of American flour and corn were imported from the
United States, which made the island further dependent economically on
that country.[79]

The desire of El País was to reduce the import duties on food of first
necessity to make the life of the poor easier. This was recommended on
such articles as flour, corn, lard, and codfish. It also recommended that
the heavy transit duty be abolished, on the ground that it might destroy the
trade itself. El País was arguing with the Boletín Mercantil over that matter. The latter believed that high transit duties would not stop American

goods from coming to Puerto Rico, while El País held the contrary opinion. The liberal paper remarked that if a war should break out between the United States and England, Puerto Rico would be in a very difficult spot because the high import and transit duties would further discourage commerce with Puerto Rico and the island would be virtually blockaded.[80]

In 1896 El País considered the United States the wealthiest nation in the world and the best and most natural market for Puerto Rican products. When war seemed imminent between the United States and Great Britain over Venezuela and the American government called for a loan there was great competition among the foreign bankers to cover it. However, the paper remarked, there was some probability that this question might have a peaceful solution but that so far the situation appeared anything but tranquil. Therefore, it was urged that the Spanish government do something about the food supply of Puerto Rico and the army in Cuba as a measure of preparedness. Dependence on the United States as the source of food was recognized but, in the opinion of the press, no one was to blame except the Spanish government. Due to transit, importation, and customs duties, absurd fiscal legislation, and legal barriers the central government had made the island dependent upon the great markets and foodstuffs of the Northern Republic. Therefore, if there were any interruption in commercial relations between Puerto Rico and the United States it would almost be as bad as a naval blockade for the island.[81]

It was pointed out that two-thirds of the food of Cuba and about one-half of that of Puerto Rico came directly from the United States in exchange for sugar and tobacco. What, the paper asked, would the Antilles do with their products and what would they do for food in case of war between England and the United States? El País urged the Spanish government to take care of the islands in view of that eventuality. It warned that England would immediately try to blockade the United States and to impede the commerce between the Antilles and that nation. England, said the paper, well knew the Achilles heel of the Yankee people. That was business. England would try to harm the business of the United States and in doing so would harm the welfare of the Antilles. To prevent that situation the paper recommended that franchises be granted in order to stimulate trade between the Antilles and Spain. By doing that the paper felt the islands would be relieved to some extent of their dependence upon the United States for flour, fats, and other food which came almost exclusively from the North.[82]

When the United States asked the European nations to participate in the Chicago Exposition the same commercial dependence was illustrated, although in a less marked degree. Of course, it was explained that Spain could not refuse the request, not only because of the position that she held in the great nations but also due to the fact that she was the nation that had discovered and civilized the New World. The Mother Country had been moved by the profound sympathy manifested by the United States during the Madrid Fair and the Barcelona Exposition when that country spent great sums of money in order to make its exhibit a success. What was to be the part of Puerto Rico in this Columbian Exposition? The press thought it unusual if Spain, Cuba, and the European nations should play a brilliant part at the Fair and Puerto Rico should remain indifferent to the great movement of modern progress. If Puerto Rico did nothing it was felt that the insular government would be guilty of ignorance of its duties to Puerto Rican history, agriculture, and industry.[83]

La Correspondencia de Puerto Rico considered the importance of the Fair to Puerto Rico in the following way: it would afford Puerto Rico an

opportunity to exhibit her products, it would inform the world of the state of
the insular civilization, and it would permit the nations to compare Puerto
Rican products with those of other tropical countries. If those reasons were
not enough to convince the government of the necessity of Puerto Rico's ex-
hibiting at the Fair, there was still another and more important reason, in
the opinion of the paper. That was the existence of the Commercial Treaty
with the United States which made Puerto Rico a pawn of the United States.
As a result of that condition it was believed that the government should do
its utmost to increase and consolidate mercantile relations with the Northern
Republic. Since the United States was the principal market for Puerto Rican
sugar and molasses the paper urged the authorities to attend the Fair in order that the Union should know of the superior qualities of the insular products.[84]

The Treaty of Reciprocity lasted from 1892 to 1894 and was never
very popular in Puerto Rico. Foreign papers were very free with their advice as to what course Puerto Rico should pursue in its economic difficulties.
They commented that, due to the mania of the United States to control everything, that that nation would not revise the commercial treaty willingly unless the terms were to be more favorable to the United States. The salvation
of Spain, according to the French press, was to make reciprocity treaties
with the South American nations and in that way form an economic union
which would reduce the importance of the United States in Spanish commerce.[85]

The Boletín Mercantil attacked the new treaty on the grounds that every
time a new law of commercial relations was made Puerto Rico was the loser.
It felt the pretext for the treaty was that of assuring Puerto Rico of a market
for its sugar. The real purpose, according to the paper, was to assure the
Yankees of a market for any merchandise that they thought convenient to
send to the island without giving a commensurate benefit in return. It was
noted that the United States still consumed the same amount of sugar after
the treaty as before and Puerto Rico lost revenue, due to the free importation of industrial goods from the United States. That situation, in the eyes
of the paper, was intolerable.[86]

A liberal paper had much the same idea. It felt that the entire direction of commerce was now with the United States and detrimental to Puerto
Rico. It asked if the other papers had thought about the danger of commercial exclusivism threatened by the reciprocity treaty. That new danger was
believed to be conducive to utter dependence on the United States. No matter how they looked at the reform, the result always appeared the same to
that paper and some of its friends---an advantage only for the Yankee commerce and production. These papers wondered what country's welfare Spain
was trying to promote by such a policy. Was it by any chance the Yankee
nation.[87]

Rafael María de Labra agreed in principle with the editorial of El
Clamor del País. He further pointed out that the capricious collection of
the customs, restrictions placed on the exportation of Puerto Rican tobacco
to the United States, and the export taxes levied on Puerto Rican products
going to Spain did much to harm the prosperity of Puerto Rico. Those, according to him, contradicted the theory of equality of the colony with Spain,
in addition to reducing the amount of insular exports to the United States.
He believed that those points were imprudent and would shortly cause
trouble between Puerto Rico and the Mother Country and would also cause
a rapprochement between the Antilles and the United States. He urged that
reforms be made before the loyalty of the long-suffering Puerto Rican people might be strained. One reform, naturally, was the abolition of export

taxes. Another was the use of more care in the making of new taxes in order that the industries of Puerto Rico should not be harmed. He also urged that Spain should follow the example of England in the collection of taxes in order that businessmen would not have to leave their businesses for several days when taxes were to be paid.[88]

The treaty with the United States was regarded by many as the principal cause for the economic decadence of Puerto Rico after 1892. The Boletín Mercantil urged that the Chamber of Commerce of San Juan should ask Spain to "repeal that treaty immediately and to make a new one in which the basis would be equality and justice."[89] It was felt that the Yankees had been quite shrewd when they made the treaty and that Puerto Rico had gained little by it. The press suggested that the governor study whether the United States could dispense either with the huge amount of sugar purchased from Cuba and Puerto Rico or with the markets for the northern industrial products that that republic enjoyed in the Antilles. In so far as the island of Puerto Rico was concerned, it was suggested that Spain make a treaty with England in order that the Puerto Rican sugar could be exported to Canada.[90]

The Chamber of Commerce of San Juan criticized various phases of the new treaty. It was pointed out that the tax on imported silk was so high that very little of that article would be imported into the island. However, it was felt that since neither Spain nor the United States grew silk and therefore did not compete in that respect, there was no justification for a rise of one hundred and ninety-eight per cent in some cases on the importation of that article. Equity, the paper said, demanded that such a duty be reduced.[91]

Another phenomenon, according to the paper, was that books or proofs printed in Europe paid more duty than those printed in the United States. The authorities claimed that they were merely trying to protect the copyrights of the authors, but the paper felt that the tariff was not the legitimate means for fulfilling or enforcing the literary copyright laws. It believed that there was always the danger of appearing as though Puerto Rico were trying to protect and foster a foreign language to the detriment of the Spanish. Such a policy was inexplicable to the paper. It warned that the time might come when that privilege would be converted into a monopoly with no benefit to the nation and with a grave danger to the Castilian language. Pulp for the manufacture of paper, building wood, and furniture also entered the island free of duty, much to the injury of insular income.[92] Even pictures from the United States paid less duty than those from Spain. That prompted one paper to ask which nation was the Mother Country.[93]

In general, the main criticism of the economic treaty was that Puerto Rican revenue had declined. Most of the American imports that previously had paid duty were admitted free of taxes into the island by virtue of the reciprocity treaty. Of course, that had an adverse effect on the insular income and the island was experiencing deficits. It is to be held in mind that the province of Puerto Rico had a separate budget from the Mother Country and that any legislation which reduced that income would not be made up by the central government. Most papers joined in the denunciation of a treaty which decreased the revenue of the island.[94]

There were rumors in 1893 that the reciprocity treaties made by virtue of the tariff law of 1890 might be annulled by the United States. These rumors were due to the alleged infringement on the part of Spain upon the commercial treaty of 1892. The New York Tribune, however, declared that such drastic action as annulment would not be necessary. That paper believed that a mere show of force would bring the Spanish government to its senses and would restore the normal operation of the treaty. As a precedent the paper cited an incident that occurred during Cleveland's first administration. At that time Spain violated the agreement relative to the equality of flags in Cuban territorial waters. All that was necessary to bring back the status quo was a strong presidential proclamation which threatened a naval demonstration in the Caribbean. Such a procedure, in the opinion of the Tribune, could be followed in the present economic difficulty.[95]

There was a great deal of mutual recrimination among the various papers concerning the treaty. The conservative papers took a holier than thou and "I told you so" attitude and at the same time called the Autonomist press unpatriotic on the grounds that that press favored the treaty before it was signed.[96] La Balanza stated that it foresaw the inconveniences and ill effects of the treaty which, it said, were coming true. [97]

In 1893 everyone from ex-deputies of the Spanish Cortes to Cuban journalists were advising the Spanish government on the best methods for getting more concessions from the United States. The Panic of 1893 was deemed the opportunity of Spain in that respect. The well being of Cuba was contrasted with the bad economic conditions prevalent in the United States during that year. Spanish opportunism was justified on the grounds that the United States did the same thing to Spain and her possessions when the Antilles were under the threat of the McKinley Bill and the United States was very prosperous.[98]

In 1893, then, the conditions were reversed, and it was urged that Spain should follow the same course as previously blazed by the United States in order to make the Spanish government amenable to concessions to the Northern Republic. Now that the United States was in need of all the foreign trade it could get, it was proposed that Spain should announce that it would greatly increase trading tariffs on the products of those countries that refused to enter into friendly negotiations. With that threat it was felt that the American industrial and agricultural producers would force their government to consider new trade terms. But, it was warned, the whole procedure should be carried out with care lest the Washington government annul the sugar franchise and the Antillean sugar would be in a worse condition than before the treaty of 1892.[99]

Ermelindo Salazar, ex-deputy of Cuba to the Cortes and a resident of Puerto Rico in 1893, stated that he was going to give, gratis, his opinion and criticisms on the commercial treaty between Spain and the United States. He said that generally treaties were made because of the necessity of finding markets for products of the signatory parties but that the decisive point of such treaties was that of concessions for mutual benefit. If they did not fulfill that consideration there was no material or moral justification for the treaty. In his opinion that consideration was not fulfilled in the reciprocity treaty of 1892 with the United States. Under pressure of threats made by that nation to close her ports to all sugars and molasses from the Antilles, Spain was forced to sign that treaty. The central government had to accept the conditions that the Yankees presented which, according to the ex-Deputy, gave the United States the lion's share of the benefits and was very harmful to the Antilles. However, he felt that since those treaties were not everlasting and since he was positive that Cleveland's government was going to amend the treaty in a way favorable to Antillean interests because such was the policy of the Democratic party, a better day was in sight for the Spanish possessions in the Caribbean.[100]

In another article Salazar suggested that if the American government should place Puerto Rico in the position of asking for the annullment of the treaty and looking for other markets or continuing with the old treaty, Puerto Rico should ask for annullment. He pointed out that Canada could furnish the same necessary articles that Puerto Rico was buying from the United States. He knew that this was a sensible alternative because he had seen Canadian products which were of excellent quality at the Columbian Exposition. His advice well illustrated the dangers that Puerto Rico would encounter if the Spanish government followed his suggestions. The facts of the case did not justify his well-intentioned but fallacious counsel. He spoke of Canada as being a great country whose population exceeded twenty millions and therefore a good place to develop as a market for Puerto Rican products. According to him Canada had many good Atlantic ports, sugar refineries, and industries. All of those factors, he said, made Canada an ideal market. In addition there was no competition from sugar-cane or sugar-beets. To clinch his arguments he stated that it was high time that Puerto Rico throw off its dependence on Cuba and the United States and turn to Canada.[101]

Why had the United States passed the McKinley Bill and forced Spain to sign a disadvantageous treaty? That was the question that the Puerto Rican papers wanted answered. One paper gave as its considered opinion two reasons: the influence of the sugar producers of Louisiana and the desire of the federal government to help the sugar-beet growers. The bill in its final form, according to the majority of the press, did more. It helped American agriculture, manufacturing, and commerce as well as the beet and cane industries.[102] Other reasons were given which were not of a commercial character. One was that the North American senators were so interested in their own welfare that they accepted bribes from the sugar trust to favor sugar legislation.[103] The conservative press cited the special interests of those senators as a reason for their obstruction of any reform in the reciprocity treaty which would decrease the profits of the Sugar Trust.

The New York Herald was quoted as substantiation of that point. That American paper stated that reform had taken a scandalous aspect, due to the lobby maintained in Washington by the Wall Street sugar syndicate which had tried to bribe various senators. It was hoped that the insinuations against the members of that high body were only gossip. Nevertheless the paper felt that for such rumors to exist was scandalous and deplorable because it tended to shake the confidence of the public in their legislators. If those charges were correct the Herald recommended that the guilty men immediately be impeached. The paper ended its article by saying that the behavior of the Senate in such an important matter must not only be above suspicion but also free from any rumors of scandal.[104]

There were various signs evident in the Puerto Rican press during 1894 showing that the Commercial Treaty of 1892 would live but a little while longer. Many protests were registered by American ship captains at the American consulate in Puerto Rico relative to the unfair enforcing of certain clauses of the treaty.[105] La Correspondencia de Puerto Rico blamed the lack of railroads, roads, and good government as well as excessive duties and the "ruinous treaty with the United States" for the disturbed economic situation of 1894.[106] Besides, it said, Puerto Rico was not even consulted when the treaty was signed and consequently needs particular to the island were ignored by the Spanish government.[107] La Democracia felt that the consumer would be affected by the breaking of the treaty in a general rise of food prices which would make the lot of the poor man worse than ever.[108] El Buscapié was of the same opinion and urged that some provisional arrangement be made with the United States concerning

the admission of foodstuffs from the North.[109] If that were not done, it predicted that food monopolies would result, the prices would sky-rocket, and
the whole country would suffer. The main sufferers of the situation, it felt,
would be the middle and lower classes whose condition was already bad
enough without adding to their difficulties.[110]

Before the final denunciation of the treaty there were many reviews of
the history of the commercial agreement with the United States. It was recalled that many people had predicted Puerto Rico was going to suffer as a
result of the treaty. After the agreement was signed those prophets appeared
correct in their predictions. The income of Puerto Rico had diminished and
her Customs House lost much revenue. It was stated that Puerto Rico was
neither consulted nor heard before the treaty was signed which joined her
economic future with that of Cuba. The point behind this controversy was
that Cuban and Puerto Rican interests had been confused when those interests were very different and even opposed.[111]

It was further remarked that the legislation between 1881 and 1891 had
been directed to bring to completion two great principles of Puerto Rican
economics. They were (1) coastal trade with Spain and (2) the suppression
of duty on the foreign traffic. Those principles were about to be realized
when the United States forced Spain to sign the disastrous commercial treaty. Spain, according to the paper, was obliged to study the North American
threat of closing American markets to the Antilles and came to the conclusion that the Yankee market was a matter of life and death to the sugar producers of Cuba and Puerto Rico. The reciprocity treaty was the logical result.[112] The chief complaint concerning the attitude of the United States in
commercial relations was that the republic did not like to make concessions
to foreign nations. A Puerto Rican paper observed that the best way to obtain concessions was to make them but apparently the United States did not
think that way.[113]

By 1894 a leading Puerto Rican paper was disillusioned as to American political parties and their platforms touching upon trade relations. It
was recalled that the Democrats came to power pledged to a program of
lowering the tariff, a program which was especially aimed against the Mc-
Kinley Bill. Salazar, the ex-Deputy from Cuba to the Spanish Cortes, went
on record as having great faith in the promises made by Cleveland's party
to do something about the McKinley Bill.[114] By 1894 the Boletín Mercantil
had taken a completely opposed viewpoint. It stated that experience had
taught Puerto Rico that in the United States political parties came to power
with a platform which was never fulfilled. That, it said, was exactly what
had happened with the Democratic party. That provided the paper with an
opportunity to give a brief resumé of the economic-political history of the
United States in recent years. Blaine and his Zollverein was cited. Next
came McKinley, who looked over the great incomes and possibilities of
those nations and worked to exploit their resources for the benefit of the
moneyed class of the United States. It was felt that he used the Monroe
Doctrine for that end.[115]

The United States was called the country of great surpluses. That
name seemed deserved when cablegrams laconically but expressively informed the Puerto Rican papers that the debt of the United States had been
reduced some fourteen million dollars in one month, which circumstance
permitted the Secretary of the Navy to construct new cruisers. The Mc-
Kinley Bill was voted and all the sugar producing countries, including Germany and all the nations with sugar colonies, hastened to make reciprocity
treaties among themselves or with the United States. The result was that

the treasury of the Union lost some sixty million dollars but the Yankee export trade had greatly increased. Afterwards came the metallic and industrial crisis of 1893 when gold fled the country. The debt went up instead of going down as was the tradition of the Model Republic during that century. One way to help solve the situation was to repeal the silver purchase act, but the silver producing states threatened energetic action if such a step were taken. Finally, when the panic became general, Cleveland forced the repeal of that silver bill. The federal government had to borrow money, strikes spread and became violent, and the Democratic party under the influence of Wilson* became convinced that tariffs were the only answer to the economic difficulties. That proposition, in the eyes of the Puerto Rican press, was a foolish proposal because it would decrease trade, not increase it. If the McKinley Bill were absolutely annulled through such actions, the Puerto Rican press favored a new treaty. It was pointed out that the position of Cuba and Puerto Rico were much different under the existing reciprocity agreement because Puerto Rico always had an adverse balance of trade. Cuba, on the other hand, always had a favorable balance. The paper urged that a new treaty be made to correct this situation.[116]

As has been mentioned before, the concessions made to the United States in the reciprocity treaty decreased the annual income of Puerto Rico. A conservative paper pointed out that the United States had never been a market for Puerto Rican tobacco and coffee and urged the Spanish government to do something to save those provincial industries. France and Germany desired the same concessions that had been granted to the United States, and it was felt that those two countries could do more for the insular industries than the United States had done under the terms of the treaty.[117] It was believed that the United States had not fulfilled the treaty in good faith because the consumption of Puerto Rican tobacco remained much the same after two years of the treaty's duration. Sugar was the only favored Puerto Rican product in the trade situation.[118]

Even the Boletín Mercantil read "with sorrow" the fact that the Democratic party was losing ground in American public opinion in 1894 and was in danger of being discredited. The main reason for that was said to be the silver question, as the United States was sharply divided on that point. It was felt that if Mr. Cleveland and his party were not able to stop agitation relative to the tariff he would lose prestige in the country as a whole. The Republicans would then gain ground, to the great delight of the monopolies, trusts, and champions of protection.[119] The main hope of the paper in case the ambitions of the Republicans were realized was an agreement with Canada. If the reciprocity treaty were annulled it was hoped that the refineries of Montreal and Quebec would take over the work then being done by the refineries of the United States. The paper regretted the apparently hopeless situation of the Democrats which was from any (meaning the Puerto Rican) point of view deplorable. Not only did it threaten the economic future of Puerto Rican sugar but it prevented the publication of the customs' reforms by the Minister of Ultramar who could do nothing until the United States had made definite tariff decisions.[120]

The customs' duty question in the United States occupied the attention of the Puerto Rican press during the latter part of 1894. It was noted with

---

* William Lyne Wilson, 1843-1900; American educator and Democratic legislator; president of the University of Virginia, 1882; Member of the House of Representatives, 1882-1894; Postmaster-General under President Cleveland, 1895; president of Washington and Lee University, 1897-1900.

regret that the conference of both houses of Congress had resulted in a complete disagreement. President Cleveland's stand on the matter was given wide approval in Puerto Rico. He was pictured as an honorable man who was trying to redeem the name of his party in spite of the internal dissensions of the Democrats. The actions of Senator Gorman* during his campaign were not felt to be consonant with fair play, because he had used Mr. Cleveland's name in a very disrespectful manner in discussing the sugar tariff question.[121]

In August of 1894 some of the commercial houses of San Juan received cables announcing that, beginning in September, sugars imported into the United States would have to pay duty because the American Senate had so decided. It was hoped that President Cleveland would veto the law which was so diametrically opposed to the platform of his party. The very passing of the law, however, was felt to be indicative of the complete failure of the Democratic economic policy. Even with the imposition of duties the paper believed that Puerto Rico would not lose the United States as a market for sugar because of the great demand for that product in the North, a product which the republic could not supply from its own fields. Another optimistic touch characterized the Puerto Rican comment on this development. That was the thought that now the Antilles would collect the customs revenue which the reciprocity treaty had denied them. It was stated that it was very annoying that those countries which enjoyed such powerful economies refused to adopt some fixed commercial policy that would promote the commercial development of its near neighbors.[122]

The actions which occurred in the American Senate during the debate on the new economic policy were considered scandalous. The American press claimed that the Sugar Trust had paid many Congressmen to vote for laws favorable to the strong league of refiners. Fifteen thousand dollars was said to have been the price of each senator. A further discredit to the Democrats was the Sugar Trust's heavy contributions to the campaign funds of that party. The Puerto Rican press lamented that state of affairs because the Democratic party was the only party which had enjoyed the confidence of Puerto Rico. It had risen to power in 1892 with a program sympathetic to the interests of the Antilles, but due to political maneuvering and the breaking of party pledges little of a constructive nature had been realized. In the opinion of the Puerto Rican press that party had fallen into the same vices as their adversaries, the Republicans, whom they had attacked with such great violence in 1892.[123]

The conservative press denounced vehemently the propaganda prevalent in the United States prior to the Wilson-Gorman Act and the breaking of the reciprocity treaty of 1892. The arguments of the American protectionists were that the country was on its way to ruin due to reciprocity and that both Puerto Rico and the United States would gain more by protection.[124]

The protectionist argument, naturally, received harsh criticism at the hands of the island's press. There were other indications in the United States that the treaty was nearing the end of its much criticized life. The United States claimed that more than four million pesos in excess had been charged by the Cuban and Puerto Rican authorities upon American imports. The American government demanded the return of that amount. That immediately produced a heated reply on the clause in the treaty touching Puerto

---

* Arthur Pue Gorman, 1839-1906; active in Maryland Democratic politics; U. S. Senator from Maryland, 1893, 1902; opposed the Force Bill of 1889; took part in the reframing of the Wilson Tariff Bill in 1894.

Rican tobacco. It was asked just what had insular tobacco gained from the treaty.[125]

It seemed that the Yankees were doing their best to destroy Puerto Rican industry and finance. First came the unfulfilled expectations relative to tobacco and then the claim for four million pesos. It was felt that Puerto Rico had a just right to ask for the denunciation of the reciprocity treaty in view of those circumstances. It was recalled that Puerto Rico had an unfavorable balance of trade and, furthermore, the island was trading in the wrong direction. Puerto Rican markets, according to the press were mostly in Europe and not in the United States. Therefore, let a new treaty be made.[126]

When the Wilson-Gorman Act was finally passed, the Spanish government declared the commercial treaty of 1892 broken in so far as it applied to the Antilles. The Minister of Ultramar, Becerra, acted hastily; even the conservative papers agreed on that. It was reflected that that minister had developed to an extraordinary degree the habit of making mistakes which divided the island against itself. The Puerto Rican sugar grinding period was over and the sugar planters were in the midst of the process of selling their crop to the United States when the peremptory order of Becerra arrived (in August of 1894) to apply the highest duties against American products immediately. That, naturally, resulted in the immediate application of high American tariffs against Antillean products. It was reflected that the Wilson-Gorman Act would not have affected the sugar production of Puerto Rico until the first part of 1895. Therefore, Puerto Rican producers would have had time to sell their crop in the United States under the terms of the old treaty and to look around for new markets. However, the arbitrary action of Becerra changed all that. Puerto Rican landlords were now in the unfortunate position of having all their 1894 sugar crop on their hands and no market in sight. Another ill effect of Becerra's action was an immediate rise in price of all foodstuffs in the island to the discontent and misery of the poor people. The abrupt action of the Minister was felt to be the work of the ministers and officials who were wholly ignorant of the interests and problems of the Antilles.[127]

El País stated that the recognized ability of the Boletín Mercantil to give reasonable appearance to the most unreasonable words had not convinced the liberals that Mr. Becerra acted with discretion when he broke the commercial treaty with the United States in such an arbitrary manner. The autonomist paper felt that Becerra had given more importance to his self-pride than to the needs and problems of Puerto Rico. It was their belief that the minister should have carefully studied the American products which could have been taxed instead of issuing a blanket order to tax all American products to the limit. As it turned out, foodstuffs in the island immediately rose in price, commercial interests suffered, and the agriculturalists were left with huge crops on their hands. The paper concluded with a remark which skirted dangerously close to treason in the eyes of the authorities. It stated that it was perfectly clear the minister had proceeded as usual without any knowledge of Puerto Rican needs, a vice typical of the centralized system attacked by the paper.[128]

"Do we win or lose by this annulment?" was the question asked by La Correspondencia de Puerto Rico. Opinion was divided. One section believed that Puerto Rico lost but that everyone was content as a result. The Yankees had been put in their place! Now, the paper continued, Puerto Rico had to face a terrible situation, the high prices of foodstuffs and the lack of immediate markets for Puerto Rican products. The reciprocity treaty had been signed without consulting Puerto Rico in 1892, and it was annulled in the same manner. The reason for that procedure, in the opinion of the paper, was that there was no public opinion in Puerto Rico to protest against such arbitrary actions. "Are we going to ruin?" was another question asked by the same paper. It was the belief of the paper that perhaps such was the case, but it observed there were some in the island who were becoming richer by the month. However, the reason given by the liberals for that situation was the existence of unjust monopolies which the government permitted to prosper at the expense of the island.[129]

The conservative papers insisted that they did not like sterile polemics which did nothing for the good of the island, but they continued to answer the liberal press in a very bombastic tone. The Boletin Mercantil asked if it was patriotic to give all the profits to the Yankees. Markets and the geographical position of Puerto Rico were not mentioned.[130] All blame was placed on the United States for having forced Spain from her 'moderate' tariff to sign the reciprocity treaty of 1892 which greatly harmed the Peninsular production.[131]

The tariff-for-revenue aspect of the Wilson-Gorman Act was not considered fair play by the insular papers. It was felt that the American government had no conscience at all in any of its actions. Therefore, the paper urged that the Spanish government had no choice other than to change the commercial routes in order to acquire from other markets those products formerly brought from the North. It was reflected that the Yankees would do the same to Puerto Rico if they could find cheaper sugar and molasses in other places than the Antilles. But, in way of consolation, the Boletín stated that the Americans were now paying double for sugar since the approval of the Wilson-Gorman Act. It pointed an accusing finger in what it considered the right direction. It advised the curious not to look to Spain or any of the other nations who had made reciprocity treaties with the United States but to the American Senate, which was the author of the new economic policy.[132].

Part III: Insular Economy after 1894

Various rumors circulated concerning the steps that Spain would take, relative to the repudiation of the reciprocity treaty. Cuba had been even more dependent upon the American market than had Puerto Rico, and it was rumored that Spain would grant the Greater Antille the privilege of making its own budget and of imposing its own duties. The reason for that, according to the report, was to avoid a commercial war between the Antilles and the United States. It was said that Spain would take care not to abandon her sovereignty and would not permit the new policy to be the first step toward the independence of Cuba. For that same reason the privilege would not include complete autonomy. The object was to give Cuba an assembly which could legislate for the island in a more advantageous manner on account of its more intimate knowledge of the economic situation. The government of Spain would reserve her right to approve the duties that Cuba would levy on American goods.[133]

The reason for the rumored privilege was that Spain wanted to preserve the American market for Cuban sugar.[134] La Correspondencia de Puerto Rico mourned that it was a pity such a beauty was a lie. It believed, as did an American paper, that it was more probable for Japan to lose the war to China than Spain to give Cuba such a privilege.[135] The <u>Boletín Mercantil</u> labelled that rumor as ridiculous because it said that not even Canada, a country that had almost an independent status, enjoyed that right. Treaties of commerce and customs, it observed, were inalienable rights of sovereignty. When the last treaty affecting the exportation of cod-fish from Canada was signed, it was England and not Canada which had been the signatory power.

The conservative paper agreed with the Minister of Ultramar that it was pure nonsense to think Spain was going to grant to any colony the right to make treaties and to fix its own duties. That, according to the paper, was the great error of the Autonomists when they befuddled the issue by placing in their program a point which it was impossible to concede. Castelar* had once characterized such a privilege as being synonomous with lowering the Spanish flag in the Antilles. The Autonomists, according to Castelar, wanted the Spanish flag to serve as a guarantee and a protection but they did not want to grant it the most elementary rights of sovereignty.[136]

Nevertheless, the liberal papers continued their appeal for some understanding with the United States which would take care of the sugar problem. It was their opinion that the economic perspective had been obscured somewhat by the Spanish government who forgot that the future of the Puerto Rican sugar industry lay with the North American Republic.[137] They stated that the sugar industry was crying for help and was looking toward the government for that aid. What was the government going to do about this call for help from a thing condemned to death? The editor remarked bitterly that everyone was writing and talking about the change to the gold standard, but no one cared anything about the sugar situation. He urged that something be done immediately about sugar because that industry was the most important source of wealth in Puerto Rico. Sugar had dropped in the market, the treaty of 1892 was broken, and the Spanish authorities appeared indifferent. The situation was bad and the liberal papers were trying to stir the government out of its habitual apathy. El Buscapié insisted that the heaven for the Puerto Rican sugar industry was the United States but that this heaven was obscured by clouds which the government should dispell. If that were done, then the labor troubles would end, the laboring classes could emerge from their misery, and prosperity would return to Puerto Rico.[138]

Liberal papers urged that there be a reform in the Spanish customs duties in order to appease the United States because that nation was of an essentially commercial character. In other words, no other language would be understood by the American government. That line of reasoning was condemned by the conservatives on the grounds that it was anti-Spanish and thus unpatriotic.[139]

El País favored some arrangement with the United States because the United States appeared to it as the only nation that could supply the quantity of articles of first necessity that the island needed. The development of the coastal trade with Spain was also favored, but the paper felt that geographical considerations prevented that trade from ever assuming a position

---

* Emilio Castelar y Ripoll, 1832-1899; a noted Spanish radical journalist, speaker, and writer; Deputy to the Cortes; active in the Spanish republic of 1868; hoped to realize the program of 1868 by evolution and legal, pacific means; for that reason he was later estranged from the majority of the republicans.

of importance. The United States was closer, its agricultural and industrial products cheaper, and the exchange as a whole more convenient. It was those considerations which prompted that paper to ask for a customs reform which would promote trade between the United States and Puerto Rico. It felt that political interests and patriotism had their place, but at the same time it favored a more rational consideration of the economic problems of the island. The paper thought that the government was following a mistaken policy when it increased the duties on American flour, thus adding to the financial burdens of the people of Puerto Rico. Spain was unable to supply all the flour that the island needed. In the opinion of the paper, articles, like flour, which were certainly classified as of the first necessity, should enjoy lesser customs duties, not for the benefit of the Yankees but for the express benefit of the Puerto Rican consumers. It referred to the high salaries of governmental officials whose offices required no hard work or special knowledge and compared that situation with the poverty stricken farmers and workers of the island who had to pay outrageous prices for the staples of life. [140]

The liberal papers blamed Spain for the adverse conditions prevalent in Puerto Rico right after the abrogation of the commercial treaty of 1892. Their point was that Spain had caused Puerto Rico to depend on American foodstuffs by virtue of the high Spanish export-import taxes. Those same high taxes on the coastal trade had driven merchants of the Antilles to find another market which would be more advantageous than Spain. The market turned out to be the United States. Therefore, the errors of the Spanish colonial administrators had resulted in the Northern Republic's being the most important market of the Antilles through no fault of Cuba and Puerto Rico.[141]

El País protested that it did not favor commercial dealings with the United States at the expense of the Mother Country. It was merely stating the facts and nothing more. Those facts were that Puerto Rico saw her most important market cut off and her interests sacrificed by the arbitrary action of Mr. Becerra. Neither Spain nor the Antilles wanted Cuba and Puerto Rico to become tributary peoples of the American mercantile sovereignty but that condition was rapidly approaching due to the inept Spanish colonial administration. Instead of arbitrarily breaking the commercial treaty El País believed that Spain should have entered into businesslike negotiations with the United States, "the celebrated land of the dollar". It felt that the Yankees would have been very receptive to trade discussions because even the most important political acts in that nation were influenced mainly by a business spirit.[142]

In regard to protectionism and its effect on the foreign and domestic policy of the United States, the Boletín Mercantil liked to consider itself as a seer and a prophet. It reminded its readers that it had warned the United States about the future ill effects of such a high tariff system, that those warnings had gone unheeded, and that now the Republican party was having to pay the price for its short-sighted policy. It was true, it said, that the sensible press of the United States had solemnly and categorically predicted that absurd protectionism could not but bring retaliation by other countries. This had happened. More, too, the people of the Union had become generally dissatisfied, and unrest had arisen. This lack of confidence in the policies of the government expressed itself first in the Congressional election of 1890 and next in the presidential election of 1892. The Republican party had been absolutely defeated. The Democratic party which had always stood resolutely against unreasonable protectionism had come to power with a great landslide. The prophesy of the paper had been fulfilled and justice

had been done to the Republicans. Cleveland, always a censor of high tariffs, was shown to be a nineteenth century Sir Galahad, as he had fought
without dismay against almost invincible elements such as governmental
influence and resources, electoral corruption from above, and even against
scurrilous attacks upon his private life. All people, seemingly, were
against the Republicans and for the Democrats.

In continuing its review of the political-economic situation, the paper
mourned that unforeseen events had destroyed the hopes of 1892 to the detriment of Puerto Rico. They were the Panic of 1893, Democratic unpopular-
ity with the electorate after 1893, and the rise of protectionist sentiment in
the United States. This had resulted in the abrogation of the commercial
treaty of 1892, for which Spain was not in the least to blame. If the liberal
papers wished to find the cause of the present economic crisis they should
turn their eyes to the north, not to the Peninsula.[143]

Agitation for some kind of a customs agreement with the United States
continued in Puerto Rico until the outbreak of the Spanish-American War.
La Democracia advised the Spanish government not to trust Depuy de Lome
with the job of negotiating a commercial treaty with the United States, because it felt that he was persona non grata to the American government.
The papers considered that war was only a remote possibility and that relations between the two nations had never been more cordial. McKinley's
words were well received. He declared that the war in Cuba should be allowed to run its course without American intervention and that only an unfortunate accident would bring about a war between the United States and
Spain. Those words were sufficient, in the opinion of the Puerto Rican
editors, to warrant agitation for closer economic relations with the United
States on the grounds that peace was assured.[144] In February of 1898 even
the conservative Boletin Mercantil was urging the government to maintain
normal relations with the United States. It advised that friendly economic
connections be maintained until war was declared and that Spain be prepared
at the same time.[145]

Caribbean countries such as Puerto Rico suffered from a single-crop
economy, which prevented the introduction of other industries. There were
two ways to improve the economic situation created by such an economy.
Commercial treaties with the United States, which would allow the Antilles
to export their agricultural products to the North in return for the necessary
industrial articles and food products, was one way of solving the economic
problem. Another method was to create new industries in Puerto Rico
which would manufacture by-products of the one great crop, sugar. This
was given intermittent study by the Spanish authorities and public-minded
Puerto Ricans. However, it usually happened that sugar rose in price just
at the time when something was about to be done concerning new industries
and the plan was shelved for the moment. The usual reliance, then, of
Puerto Rican agriculturalists was upon reciprocity treaties and not upon
native industries.

The liberals of the island wanted to develop the United States as a
market of first importance, but the conservatives were afraid of such a
procedure. The latter favored the development of a coastal trade with the
Mother Country in order to strengthen the political bonds between the Antilles and Spain. They regarded closer economic relations with the United
States as being the first steps toward political control. Such, in general,
was the situation by 1898. The see-saw of reciprocity and coastal trade
was inclining toward another commercial agreement with the United States
by the time of the war. The year 1898 ended the old political-economic

controversy and now Puerto Rico is the third best market of the United States in the world. No great industries have been developed as yet, but the island is a thriving agricultural community and absolutely dependent economically upon the United States.

(1) El Buscapié, July 30, 1894.
(2) Boletín Mercantil, August 15, 1888.
El Eco, November 10, 1895.
La Correspondencia de Puerto Rico, October 9, 1893; September 28, 1897; January 16, 1898.
(3) El Buscapié, October 4, 1891.
El Magisterio de Puerto Rico, September 28, October 26, November 16, 1890; February 1, March 15, 1891.
La Razón, August 5, November 29, 1890.
Brau, Salvador: Ecos de la Batalla, p. 147.
(4) Boletín Mercantil, November 25, 1888.
(5) El Buscapié, May 31, 1894.
(6) La Correspondencia de Puerto Rico, February 3, 1895.
El Buscapié, October 9, 1894.
El País, February 8, 1896; August 28, 1897.
(7) El País, August 28, 1897.
(8) La Correspondencia de Puerto Rico, February 9, December 30, 1895.
(9) La Correspondencia de Puerto Rico, February 9, December 30, 1895.
(10) El Eco, November 10, 1895.
(11) La Correspondencia de Puerto Rico, December 30, 1895.
(12) El Buscapié, January 1, 1893.
El Diario de Puerto Rico, August 16, 1893.
La Correspondencia de Puerto Rico, December 3, 30, 1895; February 9, 1895; April 27, 1896.
El País, January 16, 1896.
La Pequeña Antilla, January 17, 1896.
(13) La Correspondencia de Puerto Rico, October 9, 1893.
(14) El País, September 5, 1896.
(15) El País, September 5, 1896.
La Correspondencia de Puerto Rico, May 12, 1894.
(16) La Correspondencia de Puerto Rico, September 28, 1897.
(17) El Clamor del País, March 27, 1888.
(18) Boletín Mercantil, November 14, 1888.
(19) El Clamor del País, May 11, 1894.
(20) La Razón, October 21, 1890.
(21) La Razón, October 21, 1890.
Other papers during the period under consideration urged that Spain reform her customs and tax laws in favor of Puerto Rico. They were:
El Buscapié, January 31, February 28, 1892; April 10, 1896; August 21, 1895.
El País, January 4, April 23, 1896.
La Correspondencia de Puerto Rico, May 19, 1894.
La Democracia, January 10, 1895.
(22) El Buscapié, January 31, 1892; February 28, 1892.
El País, January 4, April 23, 1896.
La Correspondencia de Puerto Rico, May 19, 1894.
La Democracia, January 10, 1895.

(23) El Buscapié, September 6, 13, 1891.
    La Democracia, August 16, 24, 1894.
    Although no liberals, the editors of La Nación Española, September 10, 13, 17, 1891 and the Boletín Mercantil, May 14, 1890 admitted that some Spanish taxes were unfair.
(24) La Razón, November 13, 1890.
(25) Ibid.
(26) La Razón, November 1, 1890.
(27) Ibid, October 21, 1890; other papers agreed with La Razón on the essential practicality of U. S. policy and made reference to "America for the Americans"; they were Boletín Mercantil, June 20, 1888; March 6, November 15, 1889; July 20, October 29, 1890; April 3, 1891.
    La República, April 26, 1893.
    La Correspondencia de Puerto Rico, December 13, 1896.
(28) La Razón, October 21, 1890.
(29) El Clamor del País, August 4, 1892.
    La Razón, January 20, 1891.
    The Boletín Mercantil, March 18, 1894, stated that the Treaty was made to save Cuban and Puerto Rican sugar.
(30) La Razón, January 20, 1891.
(31) La Correspondencia de Puerto Rico, February 6, 1893.
    La Razón, November 13, 1890; January 20, 1891.
    Even the Boletín Mercantil, April 30, 1892, agreed on the necessity of the American market.
(32) La Razón, November 1, 1890.
(33) Boletín Mercantil, November 30, 1888.
(34) Boletín Mercantil, February 19, November 21, 1890.
(35) El Buscapié, February 28, 1892; January 18, 1894.
    El Clamor del País, June 30, 1892.
    Boletín Mercantil, May 14, October 29, 1890.
(36) Boletín Mercantil, October 29, December 10, 1890; February 6, 1891; October 4, 1892.
(37) Boletín Mercantil, February 21, October 29, 1890.
    La Pequeña Antilla, January 22, 1896.
    La Democracia, April 25, 1898.
    La Bomba, March 16, 1895.
    Abril, Mariano: Sensaciones de un Cronista, p. 8.
(38) Boletín Mercantil, February 21, October 29, 1890; April 3, 1891; February 26, 1893.
(39) Boletín Mercantil, February 21, October 29, 1890; April 3, 1891; February 26, 1893.
(40) La Razón, November 4, 1890.
(41) Boletín Mercantil, November 7, December 28, 1890;
    La Razón, November 4, 20, 1890.
(42) Boletín Mercantil, October 29, November 7, December 10, 1890.
(43) La Razón, November 6, 1890.
(44) Boletín Mercantil, November 9, 1890.
(45) La Razón, November 20, 1890.
    Boletín Mercantil, February 21, 1890.
(46) La Razón, November 11, 1890.
(47) Boletín Mercantil, February 6, 1891.
    La Democracia, November 3, December 15, 1896.
    La Razón, November 11, 1890.
(48) La Razón, November 13, 22, 1890.

(49) El Clamor del País, March 15, 1892.
El Buscapié, January 31, 1891.
La Razón, November 13, 1890.
Boletín Mercantil, October 29, November 7, 1890; although not a liberal, this paper agreed on the necessity of a treaty with the United States.
(51) La Razón, November 22, 1890.
(52) La Razón, September 20, 1890. (The liberal paper)
Boletín Mercantil, October 29, 1890 (conservative).
(53) La Razón, September 20, 1890.
Boletín Mercantil, May 14, June 27, 1890.
(54) La Nación Española, May 12, 1892.
La Razón, September 20, November 13, 1890.
El Buscapié, January 31, 1892; April 10, May 14, 1896.
(55) Boletín Mercantil, February 19, May 14, October 29, 1890; May 25, April 30, 1892.
La Correspondencia de Puerto Rico, February 6, 1893.
La Razón, November 11, 13, 1890; September 20, 1890.
(56) La Razón, September 30, 1890.
(57) La Razón, October 25, November 11, 25, 1890.
(58) Boletín Mercantil, May 14, 1890.
La Razón, October 25, November 1, 1890.
(59) La Razón, October 4, November 6, 11, 1890.
Other papers that agreed with La Razón but not in such an outspoken manner were:
El Clamor del País, August 20, 1891.
El Buscapié, February 28, 1892.
(60) La Razón, November 25, 1890.
(61) La Razón, September 16, 20, 1890.
The conservative Boletín Mercantil, May 14, June 27, 1890, agreed that the Spanish government was slow to act; it conceded in its numbers of April 30 and May 25, 1892 that the U.S. was the natural market of Puerto Rico.
El Diario de Puerto Rico, May 10, 1894, felt that Spain should waste no time in the making of trade treaties with the Northern Republic.
(62) Boletín Mercantil, May 14, October 29, 1890.
La Razón, November 25, 1890.
(63) Boletín Mercantil, February 1, 6, October 29, November 7, December 28, 1890; April 10, August 16, 1891; December 9, 1892.
La Razón, October 21, 1890, quotes La Balanza.
(64) Boletín Mercantil, October 29, December 28, 1890; October 4, 1892; September 10, 1893; January 18, 1895.
El Buscapié, December 12, 1894.
La Razón, November 13, 1890.
(65) La Balanza, June 11, 1893.
(66) Boletín Mercantil, November 21, 1890; November 18, December 2, 1892.
(67) Boletín Mercantil, February 19, June 27, 1890; August 16, November 6, 22, 1891; May 20, 25, December 2, 1892; May 11, 1894; January 18, 1895.
La Correspondencia de Puerto Rico, October 4, 1892; February 24, 1893.
El Buscapié, October 8, 1894.
La Balanza, June 11, 1893.
La Razón, November 11, 1890.

(68) Boletín Mercantil, February 19, May 14, October 29, 1890; April 30, May 25, 1892; March 18, 1894.
El Diario de Puerto Rico, May 10, 1894.
La Correspondencia de Puerto Rico, February 6, 1893; February 9, 1895.
La Razón, November 11, 13, 1890.

(69) Hitchcock, Frank H.: Trade of Puerto Rico, p. 26., Washington; U.S. Printing Office; 1898.

(70) Boletín Mercantil, July 1, August 5, 1891.

(71) Ibid, July 1, 1891; May 20, 1892; March 18, September 12, 1894.

(72) Ibid, April 10, 1891; January 18, 1895.

(73) Boletín Mercantil, November 6, 1891.

(74) Ibid, April 10, 1891.

(75) Boletín Mercantil, October 11, 1891.

(76) El Buscapié, January 31, 1892.
Boletín Mercantil, November 6, 1891.

(77) Boletín Mercantil, August 16, 1891; May 25, 1892.

(78) El Buscapié, January 14, 18, December 10, 1894.
Boletín Mercantil, February 13, 1895.
La Balanza, June 16, 1893.
Revista Mercantil, April 4, 1895.

(79) El Buscapié, July 30, 1894.
La Balanza, May 24, July 21, 1893.
Boletín Mercantil, September 12, 1894; February 13, 1895.
El País, January 4, 1896.
Lopez Tuero, Fernando: La Reforma Agrícola, p. 61, 91.

(80) El País, January 4, 11, 1896.

(81) La Correspondencia de Puerto Rico, February 9, December 30, 1895.
El País, January 4, September 5, 1896.
Boletín Mercantil, May 25, 1892; January 18, 1895; February 4, 1898.

(82) El País, January 4, 1896.

(83) Boletín Mercantil, December 25, 1892; April 23, 1893; February 12, 1896.
El Buscapié, January 1, 1893.
La Correspondencia de Puerto Rico, February 6, 1893.

(84) La Correspondencia de Puerto Rico, December 21, 28, 1892; January 4, 9, February 6, May 2, 12, 31, 1893; February 9, 1895.

(85) La Correspondencia de Puerto Rico, June 13, 1897.
El Buscapié, January 17, 1892; January 18, 1894.

(86) Boletín Mercantil, May 25, 1892; August 29, 1893; March 18, July 6, 1894.
El Buscapié in its article of January 22, 1894 agreed with its conservative colleague.

(87) La Correspondencia de Puerto Rico, May 19, 1894.
El Diario de Puerto Rico, March 15, 1894.
El Clamor del País, May 31, 1892.

(88) El Clamor del País, June 30, 1892.

(89) Boletín Mercantil, October 4, December 9, 1892; August 29, 1893; March 18, April 18, July 6, 27, 1894.
La Correspondencia de Puerto Rico, October 9, 1893, urged modification but not outright repeal.

(90) El Buscapié, January 22, 1894.
La Correspondencia de Puerto Rico, October 4, 1892.
Boletín Mercantil, October 4, 1892.

(91) Boletín Mercantil, December 2, 1892.

(92) Boletín Mercantil, December 9, 1892.

(93) La Balanza, March 19, 1893.
(94) El Buscapié, October 8, 1894.
La Correspondencia de Puerto Rico, February 24, 1893; May 19, 1894.
La Democracia, September 10, 1894.
Boletín Mercantil, October 4, 1892.
El Clamor del País, May 31, June 30, 1892; June 8, 1893.
La Balanza, June 4, 1893.
Lopez Tuero, Fernando: Estudios de Economía Rural, p. 106.
(95) El Clamor del País, June 8, 1893.
Boletín Mercantil, June 22, 1894.
(96) La Balanza, June 11, 1893.
El Diario de Puerto Rico, May 24, 1894.
Boletín Mercantil, June 22, 1894.
(97) La Balanza, June 11, 1893.
(98) Boletín Mercantil, August 29, 1893.
(99) Boletín Mercantil, August 29, 1893.
(100) La Correspondencia de Puerto Rico, October 9, 1893.
(101) La Correspondencia de Puerto Rico, October 10, 1893.
(102) La Balanza, April 22, 1894.
El Clamor del País, March 24, 1888; October 19, 1889; December 12, 1891.
Revista Mercantil, August 6, 1895.
Boletín Mercantil, February 6, 1891; April 10, 1891; April 30, 1892; October 21, 1894.
(103) La Balanza, April 16, 1893.
Boletín Mercantil, May 2, August 24, 1894; January 27, 1895.
(104) Boletín Mercantil, June 22, 1894.
(105) La Balanza, March 4, 1894.
El Buscapié, March 11, 1894.
(106) La Correspondencia de Puerto Rico, May 10, 1894.
(107) La Democracia, September 8, 1894.
La Correspondencia de Puerto Rico, October 23, 1893.
El Diario de Puerto Rico, May 24, 1894.
(108) La Democracia, September 10, 1894.
(109) El Buscapié, September 24, 1894.
(110) El Buscapié, October 10, December 10, 1894.
(111) El Diario de Puerto Rico, March 15, May 24, 1894.
Boletín Mercantil, December 10, 1890; November 30, 1892; September 7, November 30, 1894.
(112) Boletín Mercantil, November 30, 1892.
(113) Ibid, December 10, 1890; January 27, 1895; April 21, 1897. La Democracia, March 28, 1895, accused the U.S. of trying to become the commercial lords of the Western Hemisphere.
(114) Boletín Mercantil, July 6, September 7, October 7, 1894; January 18, 1895.
(115) Boletín Mercantil, July 6, 1894; January 27, 1895.
(116) Boletín Mercantil, July 6, September 7, 1894.
(117) La Correspondencia de Puerto Rico, May 12, 1894.
Boletín Mercantil, March 18, April 18, 1894.
(118) La Correspondencia de Puerto Rico, February 6, 1893.
Boletín Mercantil, August 29, 1893; March 18, 1894.
(119) Boletín Mercantil, April 18, 1894.
(120) El Buscapié, January 22, 1894.
La Correspondencia de Puerto Rico, October 10, 1893.
Boletín Mercantil, April 18, August 24, 1894.

(121) Boletín Mercantil, March 18, April 13, August 24, 1894; January 27, 1895.
La Correspondencia de Puerto Rico, August 13, 1894.
(122) El Buscapié, September 24, October 10, 1894.
Boletín Mercantil, August 24, 1894.
(123) Boletín Mercantil, April 4, 1888; September 26, 1890; June 8, August 24, 1894; March 8, 27, 1896.
El País, March 24, 1898, agreed with its conservative colleague.
(124) Boletín Mercantil, December 28, 1890.
(125) Boletín Mercantil, May 14, October 29, November 7, 1890.
La Correspondencia de Puerto Rico, January 16, 1894; December 13, 1896.
La Balanza, August 25, 1893.
La Razón, November 11, 13, 1890.
(126) Revista Mercantil, April 4, 1895.
Boletín Mercantil, July 27, 1894.
La Correspondencia de Puerto Rico, October 10, 1893.
(127) Boletín Mercantil, May 3, 1896.
El Buscapié, August 29, 1894.
El País, May 4, 1896.
La Correspondencia de Puerto Rico, August 29, 1894.
La Democracia, September 8, 1894.
(128) El País, April 22, May 4, 1896.
(129) La Correspondencia de Puerto Rico, August 9, 10, 29, December 18, 1894. This paper carried on a consistent attack against monopolies from September to December of 1894.
La Democracia, August 24, September 8, 1894.
(130) Boletín Mercantil, April 10, 1891; September 5, 1894.
El País, April 10, 1896, refutes the arguments of the Boletín.
(131) Boletín Mercantil, June 22, November 30, 1894; May 3, 1896.
La Balanza, February 25, 1894.
(132) Boletín Mercantil, May 2, June 22, October 7, November 30, 1894.
(133) El Buscapié, December 12, 1894; August 21, 1895.
La Correspondencia de Puerto Rico, January 7, 1895.
Boletín Mercantil, January 18, 1895.
(134) Boletín Mercantil, January 18, 1895.
La Correspondencia de Puerto Rico, January 7, 1895.
(135) Boletín Mercantil, January 18, 1895; March 6, 1898.
La Correspondencia de Puerto Rico, January 7, 1895.
(136) Boletín Mercantil, January 18, 1895.
(137) El Buscapié, January 24, 1894; August 21, 1895; April 24, November 23, 1896.
El País, March 3, 1897.
La Correspondencia de Puerto Rico, September 28, 1897.
La Democracia, February 15, 1898.
(138) El Buscapié, January 24, 1894.
(139) Boletín Mercantil, August 19, 1888; January 27, 1895.
El País, April 10, 1896.
El Buscapié, April 10, May 14, 1896.
(140) El País, April 23, 1896.
(141) El Buscapié, August 21, 1895; April 10, 1896.
El País, April 23, 1896.
(142) El País, April 22, 1896.
(143) Boletín Mercantil, March 18, June 22, November 23, 1894.
(144) La Democracia, February 15, 1898.
(145) Boletín Mercantil, February 27, 1898.

American Characteristics According to Latins

Some of the reasons why the United States gained the epithet of "Colossus of the North" were its immense size, its rapid expansion westward at the expense of all who got in its way, and its material progress. Although Latin-Americans admired the material progress of the United States, they decried all the defects that appeared in the political, social, and administrative life of the American nation. The rapidity of that progress enabled the critics of the United States to label the nation and its people as interested only in money, speed, and industrial development. This expansion had been most remarkable in the years since the Civil War. During that time the transcontinental railroads had been built, the North had become predominantly industrialized, emigration had enormously increased the population, and American businessmen had made a bid for world markets, especially in the Caribbean. All those developments were regarded as truly marvelous. Puerto Rican papers were in the habit of publishing data on that progress and marvelling how such a young nation could compete successfully with Old World powers. The United States seemed to lead the other nations in the world in civilization and progress because of its lack of business inhibitions.[1]

To some Puerto Ricans the United States appeared as a free country, a country of the Puritans who with the Bible in hand and a prayer on their lips, crossed valleys and mountains conceiving great hopes of liberty and redemption. It was thought of as a young country with powerful energies, developing with amazing rapidity. Its constitution was regarded as a monument to fraternity. Washington represented Cato and Lincoln appeared as the Redeemer. Liberty and order were pictured as the ideals of that country. Artists had made statues to both the men and the ideals. Thousands had emigrated from Europe to the promised land dreamed of by humanity. In less than a century that tribe of Puritans turned into a powerful nation which amazed the world with its inventions, progress, and respect for the law. Liberty there, according to Mariano Abril,[*] had not been won by bitter internecine warfare. Liberty had been won by the conscientious work of all the people.[2]

Liberals implied that Spain did not progress. Conservative papers retorted that Spain did progress. It was explained that peoples and nations progressed automatically. Why, then, should an old and glorious nation like Spain be disturbed by the antics of a nation that could only be classified as a newly rich aspirant anxious to be admitted into the family of nations? Besides, other factors than money must be taken into account---for example, historical achievements by the immortal Admiral and others too numerous to mention, cultural attainments in art, literature, and music.[3]

In spite of its great material progress there was no culture in the United States according to the Boletín Mercantil, because a truly cultured people would not permit the use of prisoners as guinea pigs for the electric-chair.[4] Even liberal papers protested because they thought that this was taking the name of progress in vain. If the death penalty had to be invoked there were other ways of inflicting it. Such torture as some of the early victims experienced were denounced as violating the spirit of progress.[5]

---

* Mariano Abril y Ostalo, 1862-1935; a noted Puerto Rican liberal, newspaper writer, author, poet, and statesman; Member of the Insular House of Representatives, 1904, and the Senate, 1917, 1920; Historian of Puerto Rico, 1931-1935.

That reaction to scientific progress enabled anti-American papers to begin
their articles with such titles as the following "Who doubts that the United
States is the most progressive nation of the world?" and then to continue
in the same ironical vein. It was pointed out that the advances of the United
States were industrial and scientific for the most part but that this misuse
of science reflected on that development. On one hand the Republic used
electricity for cruel executions, while Spain used it for experiments in submarine navigation. The advances of Spain were demonstrated to be in the
interests of humanity, civilization, and science. Those of the United States,
that land of Edison, which desired above all else to attain perfection in material things, had failed. Its use of electricity, by order of the law, to ex-
ecute people in a horrible way appeared as a blot on civilization. Nothing
like that had ever appeared in the history of the Inquisition.[6]

Besides, where did the United States acquire this so-called monopoly
on progress that the liberal papers seemed to attribute to it? If judged by
recent events, the United States had more of a monopoly on bungled executions, lynchings, and murders rather than progress. "Let such papers as
El Clamor del País be careful whom it calls reactionary and progressive.
Facts are the best proof."[7]

Many people speculated as to the secret of the great advance of the
United States. Something must be responsible for that advance so lacking
in other countries. Was it due to a more penetrating intellectual disposition,
some exuberant vital sap, or some aptitude for the practical which other
peoples did not have? The Americans, according to some editors, avoided
the purely theoretical, the nebulous, and hypothetical. Their parliamentary
oratory for the most part was sober, their poetry concrete, their art simple and useful, and their system of instruction adjusted to the principle of
the direct application of the practical. There the youth of the nation lost
nothing by spending so little time on his studies if one were to judge from
men like Webster and Edison. What, then, was responsible for the gigantic
enterprises so common to that country?

La Nación Española explained it by the application of three principles
to everything. They were (1) capital and the man, (2) ideas and the man,
and (3) propaganda which produced a spirit of association that was lacking
in other countries. This spirit of association may be called coöperation.
Latins have always been known for their individuality. Co-öperation has
been difficult to attain in many enterprises. The paper stated that everything was sacrificed by the North Americans for that principle, the spirit
of association. Fulton was derided in Europe. He went back to the United
States and there he found the three indispensable factors which made possible the steamship.[8] The results of the full use of collective effort or co-
öperation was best seen in the work of the Yankee people who in less than a
century developed frontier territory into a powerful and wealthy nation.
That, according to the liberal editor, was an example to be followed.[9]

It was believed that if that spirit were followed in Puerto Rico, business would improve, poverty would be lessened, and a new era of prosperity would begin. However, according to the article, routine and inertia were
the two great enemies of that spirit and would lead only to the ruin of the
nation, no matter how abundant the natural resources. Apathy, indifference,
and too much individualism were considered by the paper the evils of Puerto
Rican society. What was needed were men of courage to start enterprises
as in the North American nation. There men with ideas co-öperated with
men of capital and both became wealthy in the end.[10] The Puerto Rican
spirit of inertia was also condemned by El Buscapié, which believed that

countries could only develop through the free use of individual abilities and
initiative. It felt that the chief obstacle to progress in Puerto Rico and
Latin-American countries was their centralized governmental systems, but
the habit of shifting responsibility and of letting things go until tomorrow,
according to the paper, were great detriments to the full development of the
country.[11]

Another explanation for American progress was the climatic theory.
It was stated that there was a great contrast between the people of cold and
warm climates. In the former, life was a continuous agitation, while in the
latter it was calm. In cold countries it was as though every man had a spur
on him all the time, but in warm countries man acted as though he had a
hundred pounds to carry around on each foot. The paper stated that people
in the United States people seemed to have time for nothing; in the tropics,
there was time for everything. The cause of these habits was said to be the
climate. Cold, continued the paper, retarded the growth of plants but it accelerated the life of man. Warmth accelerated the growth of plants and retarded the vital movements of man.[12]

New York City was taken as the example to prove that contention.
There the Puerto Rican visitor was surprised to see men so active and so
prematurely old. He felt that there were few men in that city who at forty
years of age were not wrinkled, old, and bent. That was caused by the continuous search for business (according to the Puerto Rican visitor) which
tired the brain, wore out the freshness of the complexion, and dulled the
eyes. There was no time for play in that city. Sunday was just another day.
It was used to go over the past week's work and to reflect on the schedule
for the following week. Americans were felt to work, eat, and rest in a
hurry. The pleasures of the table, of relaxation, and of play were almost
unknown there, according to La Instrucción Pública. The continuous strain
under which the brain was kept made necessary the stimulus of alcoholic
drink. Liquor was taken without any consideration of the social graces.
Whether the stomach was empty or full made no difference to the North
American. He finally ended in destroying his system and in making drunk-
enness a commonplace because he had to do everything in a hurry. Progress could not wait for any iorm of reiaxation.[13]

Heat was said to produce life and also to paralyze it. That, said an
article, was why men were so indolent in warm climates. In the tropics,
rest was the occupation for man, and continuous energy was the occupation
of nature. In the cold climate man had to work hard to keep alive. It was
because of those marked differences of climate, then, that man progressed
so much in the north and not in the tropics.[14]

The difference between the Latin and American characteristics was
further explained in an article entitled "Nosotros y los Yankees" by Jesus
María Amadeo. According to him the Latin civilization took possession of
the southern continent and the Anglo-Saxon race took the northern. The
region where New York is found was savage jungle at the time of discovery,
much like the condition of South America. Why, he asked, had the northern
continent progressed so much farther than the southern when both were
nothing but wilderness at the time of discovery? Was it that the Anglo-
Saxon race was superior to the Latin? Or was it that the portion of land
occupied by the Anglo-Saxons was more fertile than the one taken by the
Latins? Those were a few of the questions asked by the writer of the article
when he compared the progress made by the Latin nation of France with
that of Spain. The climate of North and South America was compared. The
climate, tó Señor Amadeo, seemed to give the northern people a keener

sense of values than people of tropical countries had. Spaniards, accustomed to the cold and heat of Spain, went to Puerto Rico, where there was summer all the year. Perspiration and heat so weakened the Spaniard that he could work far less than he had in Spain. Therefore, people of tropical countries should appreciate the advantages enjoyed by the Anglo-Saxons in North America. The winter climate had the effect of stimulating activity, both physical and mental. Summer, however, exhausted the body and the mind, with the result that diseases that came from a weakened physical and mental condition came to Puerto Ricans earlier than to the North Americans.[15]

One reason for the anti-American attitude of the conservative papers was their fear of American liberalism, democracy, and equality. There was always the fear in the back of their minds that the example of the United States might prove too much for the people of the Antilles, who might some time begin to reason that what was good for the Americans might also be good for them. Perhaps, too, in the name of the liberalism, equality, and democracy of the late nineteenth century the United States might intervene and be supported by the liberal elements of the Spanish islands. The only way, then, to combat this possibility was to ridicule all that was American and to continue as far as possible the old Spanish colonial system in its entirety.

Puerto Ricans were not granted the same rights as the Spaniards; this condition caused constant agitation on the part of the natives for equal rights and privileges but such campaigns were stubbornly opposed by those in power. Spanish opposition was always heightened when the liberals cited the example of the United States. As a result, the Spanish government blindly refused to understand the insular point of view and classified all liberals either as separatists or annexionists.[16]

It was recommended that instead of searching for exotic institutions for the probable well-being of Puerto Rico, people should turn their eyes to the old and free Spanish institutions, in which there was no liberty to insult anyone.[17]

The Spanish government tried in vain to prohibit all kinds of rights, actions, and demonstrations and even all political thinking in the island. Puerto Rican businessmen went to the United States and saw there a progressive people to whom liberty was no danger. On the contrary, it was an incentive. Those businessmen, after viewing the operation of progress within liberty and a free morale which was not revolutionary, returned to Puerto Rico praising the American system that allowed so much progress.[18] The Spanish authorities, on the other hand, were skeptical. To them liberty and progress were merely shields behind which separation was hiding. Between progress and separatist agitation, the authorities felt there was no choice at all. The best system to them was the old colonial system, in spite of its arbitrary governors, capricious law enforcement, and feudal economic order.[19] Events like the Componte might happen. Those were unfortunate but, after all, they did not happen very often. Some might say that they had a healthful effect because they showed that there still was a government and that separatists should take care.

The North American people were shown by liberals like Fernández Juncos to have carried the concept of liberty to the highest point that it could attain. A proof of that was the fact that the Rights of Man occupied a prominent place in the Constitution of the United States. He believed the reason why the United States had made such great strides in the nineteenth century was that liberty was the rule and restrictive laws were the exception.[20]

Some writers felt that Canada, with her undesirable territory, could be happy with autonomy while Cuba and Puerto Rico, long coveted by the Yankees, would be very unhappy with such a regime. A statement like that immediately caused angry expostulations by liberal editors. It was asked why the Anglo-Saxon race was the only race in the world that could be happy with liberty whereas that same liberty would make Cubans and Puerto Ricans unhappy. There was no reason why the Anglo-Saxons should be the chosen race with the precious gift of freedom. El País believed that Latins had the same aptitudes as other races for using liberty.[21] The United States proposed to the Spanish government at various times that Cuba and Puerto Rico be granted the same kind of liberty as the English colonies. Some Puerto Rican politicians retorted "We are not English" which seemed to underestimate the Latin ability to use that liberty.[22]

Ways for imitating the United States other than the suffrage were mentioned. Manuel Fernández Juncos defended Arbor Day. His defense was· to the effect that it had an educational value for the children because, as originated by J. Sterling Morton of Nebraska, it taught children the beautiful idea of planting trees. He felt that it was a holiday which should be observed by all the world irrespective of nations and peoples. It was a recreational and purely scholarly spectacle. This reasoning was prompted by the fact that the Spanish government would favor nothing that had any political ideas or might remotely be used to disseminate revolutionary propaganda. The custom of Arbor Day had become more popular each year in the United States. Millions of trees had been planted as a result. He concluded his article by saying that Puerto Rico should adopt that custom because the island had such a wonderful climate that trees could be grown easily. It would do much to reforest the island, a project that was greatly needed in Puerto Rico since the once magnificent forests had been cut down by greedy persons.[23] Fernández Juncos was a public spirited man who at that early date saw the evils of a wasteful agricultural system. The hills of Puerto Rico, even in 1897, were being cleared of trees to make way for cane, coffee, and tobacco. The charcoal-burners were, and still are, perhaps, the worst bane of the beautiful island. Slowly and surely Puerto Rico has been denuded of trees, erosion has set in, and the rains, without the attraction of vegetation, have decreased. Fernández Juncos realized the dangers of deforestation and erosion. He urged that something be done, but since he was agitating for the introduction of an American custom, he had little hope for success with the anti-American Spanish authorities.

Another stratagem used by the conservatives in their never-ending attack upon liberalism was to cite the South American republics as examples of liberty. Many visionaries, the Boletín Mercantil said, liked to think that the name 'republic' in South America meant necessarily freedom. Here the conservative papers were standing on a little better ground than when they attacked the United States. It was easily shown that the South American republics were republican in name only and that those peoples had gained nothing by their ingratitude to the Mother Country. As for freedom of the press, examples were given of what had happened to editors who had criticized governments there. Thus the pacific and prosperous colonial period of those countries was in marked contrast to the present practice of democratic principles, in the eyes of the Boletín.[24]

Liberty and courtesy, said the conservatives, had been taught the world by the Spanish soldiers in their struggles with the Arabs, Italians, Dutch, and English. If this were not true, why did the great Velasquez paint of the courtly Surrender of Breda in the way that he did?[25]

It was admitted, however, that there were a few cultured persons in the United States in spite of what the conservatives said to the contrary. For that reason, continued the paper, the excesses of the Yankee law-makers had so little echo in the sensible opinion of a commercial and businesslike people who were by tradition little given to political adventures. It was felt that not much attention was paid to those excesses even when they came from senators.[26]

The fact that the Masonic Order could consider the founding of a co-educational university was taken as another proof of the existence of liberty in the United States. The word 'Mason' has always been productive of fear and apprehension in Old World nations and in their descendants in the colonies. Here, said El Eco, was an illustration of the length to which freedom went in that country. No longer did the word 'Mason' mean riot and revolution and plots against the government. Instead it meant education and progress. Such were the fruits of liberty![27]

Social equality in the United States sometimes took peculiar turns. An ex-mayor of New York City was sued by his barber for payment. An affair like that, a tradesman's suing an ex-mayor, was inconceivable to Latin mind. People like barbers are always paid to keep up appearances between classes in Puerto Rico. The ex-mayor seemed to be demeaning himself and his class by such an incident.[28]

It was felt that the United States was a little hypocritical in its theory and practice of democracy. That much vaunted democracy was denied to the Chinese in the United States, who were persecuted and subjected to exclusion laws. No matter how the Chinese government protested, it was all in vain. Thus, there was no liberty, equality, or democracy in the land of Washington. Arabs, Patagonians, and Armenians could enter the model republic but the poor Chinese were excluded. Now did the liberals refuse to believe that intolerance and injustice existed in the Yankee nation, the country which was the prototype of democratic peoples?[29]

Other social inequalities were pointed out by the Boletín and La Balanza. The Anglo-Saxon, said those papers, revealed his hatred for all races other than his own in his persecution of black men as well as yellow men. Therefore, that equality was illusory. The beautiful words of freedom and equality could not exist in a country with "Jim Crow" cars. Why, then, were those words used if they were not followed?[30]

The main use for those words, as explained by the conservative papers, was to beguile the lower classes so that they would support a system which was patently against them. Papers asked each other questions that were reminiscent of the eighteenth century and of the idealists of the French Revolution. La Revista asked the Boletín "Do you or do you not accept social equality?" This excursion into dialectics immediately brought up the example of the United States. It was explained that the American Union was dedicated to universal fraternity, its political principle was social equality; but practice there gave the lie to theory. The race troubles were cited as a proof. The paper concluded its round-about answer to La Revista's question by moralizing. It said that as long as the world existed and as long as there were men of vice and virtue, of sloth and industry, of folly and wisdom, there would always be a revolutionary flag to be exploited by disturbers of the peace. One such flag, then, was this much talked of social equality. Let La Revista now define its concept of social equality.[31]

Conservatives of 1889 viewed democracy in the same light as the members of the Old Regime viewed the French Revolutionaries. It was felt to be a radical doctrine fitted for young peoples. The pros and cons of its doctrines were on many lips. Conservatives said that its watchword was 'forward' although few of the converts knew in just what direction, and predicted that it would become a terrible weapon in the hands of the ignorant masses.[32]

Ignacio Díaz Caneja, editor of the Boletín Mercantil, believed that the democracy of the North would fail when the conquests of industry and commerce were finished because leisure and abundance would inevitably bring a dictatorship to preserve the progress gained.[33]

The stand that there should be liberty for criticism as well as for applause was flatly rejected by the Boletín. Applause for the government was the only purpose of expression for that paper; criticism was absurd. Besides, it was unpatriotic.[34] Articles appeared in this manner "¡La Democracia!" in reactionary papers. Attacks followed showing that democracy would yell and make a fuss about anything at anytime. Nothing was sacred to it. Kings, thrones, principles, even civilization, meant nothing to this theory of radicalism according to the 'incondicionales'. Democracy was demonstrated to be imbued with the philosophy of materialism and evil.[35]

The many attacks upon it seen in the conservative press were directed against such papers as El Clamor del País, El País, El Resumen, and the other fountains of liberalism in Puerto Rico. 'Incondicional' editors were constantly pre-occupied with the threat of liberalism or autonomy which the above mentioned papers advocated.

In the eyes of the 'incondicionales' there was only one thing responsible for that situation. That was the influence exerted by the United States on political thought. 'Incondicional' editors, therefore, considered it their sacred duty to defend all that was Spanish and to condemn all that came from the United States. Even the air was Spanish, they said, and there was no room for autonomist or pro-American thoughts. Progress must be fought, liberalism and democracy must be exposed in their 'true' light, and the equality in the Yankee nation must be shown up as the ideal rather than the real.

Salvador Brau, the editor of El Clamor del País, the most inveterate of all the liberal papers also disagreed with his colleague, Díaz Caneja. Brau believed that modern democracy, the daughter of the Renaissance and Reformation as he termed it, came to America with that handful of Puritans who founded Massachusetts and later helped to write the Declaration of the Rights of Man into the American constitution. It would not be through force or dictatorship that that American nation would be preserved, he believed, but through respect for the laws and the constitution. With respect to the relations existing between the United States and the Antilles Brau warned "It is foolish to think that the commercial relations between two countries affects only their material interests."[36] That was a prophetic warning that the Spanish government's maligning of democracy would not be enough to oppose the growing influence of the United States in the Antilles.

Nor did he believe that the strengthening of cultural and material bonds would suffice to keep Puerto Rico loyal to Spain. The hoped-for cultural and political union of the former Spanish colonies in America with Spain, he felt, was more of the imagination and dreams than of reality. Exclusivism, centralization, and the unity of conscience in the Antilles were not enough in his estimation to oppose American influence in the Western Hemisphere. The North American democracy had as its basis individual liberty and that could not be fought with tyranny, superstition, traditional doctrines, or past glory. Its interpretation was the same in any part of the world regardless of race or nation. Age old repression could not defeat democracy or liberty. History had proven that. Torquemada* had not defeated Luther, the Syllabus had not overcome Fulton, and the glory of Washington and Franklin overshadowed the force of the Duke of Alva or Philip II. Therefore, Brau stated, if Spain wanted to continue her existence in the New World she had to recognize the new forces of liberty, equality, and democracy.[37]

The American spirit of democracy was neatly put by Braschi at the time that a new state was admitted into the Union. No doctrine or tradition had prevented that. When he saw a country ruled by a democratic regime, where the Protestant enemies of the infallibility of the Pope were in the majority, where there were no kings and princes, where stars were added to its flag, and where the treasury was full of money, he asked himself "Is that republican regime so bad as they say it is?"[38] Needless to say, that kind of reasoning did little to increase his popularity with the Spanish government.

'Compontes' were something that did not occur in the United States. This was supported by the history of Jefferson Davis after the American Civil War. The chief of the Confederacy was brought to a trial which lasted a long time, and that fact, according to the paper, was the salvation of Davis. The length of the trial permitted reason to prevail over wartime hatred. President Johnson was appreciated for his greatness and political astuteness in that case because he did not surrender to post-war prejudice. He was shown to be a man determined that his government should commit no mistakes in spite of the mistakes committed by the late Confederacy. He did all that he could to cool the intransigent spirits so as to consolidate the peace and to make impossible any future disturbance or attacks against the unity of the nation. For that, it was considered, he deserved the applause of the civilized world. No 'Componte' was permitted to revive and to intensify political hatreds. On the contrary, conciliation was in order.[39]

When the United States decided to rearm at various times in history, the size of the appropriations and the way that they were approved were sources of wonder to foreigners. In the first place, a mere representative proposed the budget in question. European representatives would never have had that much power, even had that representative been the president of the budget commission. It was admitted that Mr. Cannon, the one who presented the budget, had a conference with the president and the cabinet beforehand, but the procedure was still inexplicable.[40] It was explained that the reason for such conduct was that in the United States there was neither a president of ministers nor a group of ministers in the parliamentary sense of the word as in Europe. Instead, there were only secretaries of each department who had not even the right to enter the House of Representatives to support his departmental budget. It was pointed out that the president could not be stopped by his cabinet, because the cabinet positions depended on him. In Europe cabinet members had more influence and could attack their leader in the newspapers. That was unheard of in the United States. The secretaries could not plot the deposition and fall of the president because the presidential power was full and complete in so far as the cabinet was concerned.[41]

* Tomas de Torquemada, 1420-1498; Spanish Inquisitor-General; distinguished for his religious zeal and relentless fight against heresy; took a prominent part in the expulsion of the Jews from Spain.

The Puerto Rican had many and varied opinions of American charac-teristics, some of which were more outstanding than others. The American was thought to be a progressive, eminently practical, resourceful person. He was believed devoted to the principles of liberty, equality, and democracy. Those principles, naturally, were considered dangerous by the conservatives and were admired by the liberals. Political parties received a judgment the same as the individual American. For example, the Republican was believed the party with the most advanced and radical ideas. The Democratic party was judged conservative and one most likely to co-öperate with foreign nations.[42] Bryan was the exception among the Democrats. The American government and its operation, then, was judged in the light of all those considerations and a rather confused picture was presented to the Puerto Rican reader if he read all the insular newspapers of the era.

(1) El Clamor del País, July 28, 1888.
     Newspaper accounts that seemed to prove the American lack of business inhibitions were as follows: stories concerning Coney Island, El Clamor del País, June 2, 1888; contests for ugly men, La Balanza, June 14, 1894; Jay Gould and his financial machina-tions, La Correspondencia de Puerto Rico, May 21, 1893; enter-prises as "The World Beater Matrimonial Company, La Corre-spondencia de Puerto Rico, February 12, 1895; and the attempt of an American to rent the bones of Columbus for display in a side-show, Boletín Mercantil, August 15, 19, 23, 26; September 23, October 5, 1888.
(2) Abril, Mariano: Sensaciones de un Cronista, p. 8.
(3) Boletín Mercantil, April 11, 1888; March 19, 25, 1890; December 12, 1890.
     La Democracia, March 12, 1891.
(4) Boletín Mercantil, August 22, November 30, 1890; June 14, 1889; January 22, 1893.
(5) La Razón, August 28, 1890.
     El Buscapié, August 31, 1890.
(6) Boletín Mercantil, August 22, 1890.
     La Balanza, May 24, 1893.
(7) Boletín Mercantil, January 13, 1888; August 25, October 2, 1889; July 23, 1891.
(8) La Nación Española, April 24, 1892.
(9) El Buscapié, June 3, 1894.
(10) La Nación Española, April 24, 1892.
(11) El Buscapié, June 3, 1894.
(12) La Instrucción Pública, January 5, 1888.
(13) La Instrucción Pública, January 5, 1888.
     Further references to the accelerated tempo of American life may be found in the following: Boletín Mercantil, June 16, 1889; La Correspondencia de Puerto Rico, December 19, 1890; El País, February 16, 1895; El Liberal, April 5, 1898; La Balanza, June 23, 1893; and El Buscapié, September 21, 1890.
(14) Ibid.
(15) El Diario de Puerto Rico, May 7, 1894.
(16) La Razón, May 8, 1890.
     Boletín Mercantil, March 30, 1890; June 28, 1891; January 3, 1892; March 1, 1893.
(17) Boletín Mercantil, March 27, 1896.
(18) Brau, Salvadro: Ecos de la Batalla, pp. 52-54.

(19) Ibid.
(20) El Buscapié, May 17, 1894.
(21) La Correspondencia de Puerto Rico, November 22, 1897.
(22) Ibid.
(23) El País, May 3, 1897.
(24) Boletín Mercantil, July 26, 1891.
(25) Ibid.
(26) El Eco, June 18, 1896.
(27) Boletín Mercantil, March 7, 1897.
(28) Ibid, April 29, 1892.
(29) Boletín Mercantil, July 17, 1889; September 3, December 10, 1890; April 24, 1892.
     La Democracia, February 5, 1895.
(30) Boletín Mercantil, April 22, 29, 1888; October 23, 27, 1889; November 22, 1889; March 1, 1893; July 20, 1894; November 3, 20, 27, 1895; September 20, 27, 1896; January 30, 1898.
     La Balanza, February 12, 1893.
(31) Boletín Mercantil, June 24, 1891.
(32) Boletín Mercantil, May 10, 1889.
(33) Díaz Caneja, Ignacio: Waterloo Político, p. 16.
(34) Boletín Mercantil, April 26, 1889.
(35) Ibid, April 4, 1888.
(36) Brau, Salvadro: Ecos de la Batalla, p. 262.
(37) Brau, Salvadro: Ecos de la Batalla, pp. 7-9.
(38) La Razón, February 25, 1890.
(39) El Clamor del País, February 18, 1888.
(40) El Liberal, April 16, 1898.
(41) Ibid.
(42) Boletín Mercantil, December 22, 1889.
     El Buscapié, May 17, 1894.
     El Clamor del País, October 30, 1895; January 26, 1898.
     La Razón, May 8, 1890.
     El País, August 24, 1897.
     La Correspondencia de Puerto Rico, December 5, 1897.

Conclusion

The Puerto Rican press reaction to the United States during the period 1888-1898 was most intense in three main fields of decreasing importance---economic, political, and cultural. The economic influence, in the eyes of the conservatives, was the most dangerous because it was the hardest to fight. When a people's purse is concerned, its political beliefs are more easily influenced. The single-crop economy of the island made it imperative that a steady market be found. That market was the United States, because Spain could by no stretch of the imagination consume all the products of Puerto Rico. Money, markets, and invisible investments did not follow political channels, in spite of what the 'incondicionales' might say or do. To them, those factors represented the insidious working of the American penetration in Puerto Rico that had to be fought incessantly.

Political propaganda, American governmental institutions, and separatist or annexionist agitators were something else. All of those influences were tangible, understood, and could be fought in the open. The conservatives could use the sordid elements of American characteristics, political actions, and foreign policy to good advantage. The liberals were instructed that Americans as a whole had no morals, either in business or in politics. Did not dollar diplomacy and the economic character of Blaine's Pan-Americanism prove the former? As for the latter, what about the condition of the poor Indians, negroes, and Chinese in the Model Republic? Besides, there was always the Monroe Doctrine to fall back upon in order to prove that the Monroe Doctrine was merely a modernized version of Manifest Destiny with a southward direction.

Considering the situation as a whole and the persistent attempts of the Spanish government to maintain a colonial system that had long outlived its usefulness, one is constrained to ask "Just what were the main influences of the United States upon Puerto Rico?" The answer must be that the most important American influence was the economic because it was founded upon geography, the complementary character of Puerto Rican-American trade, and the enormous wealth of the United States which was looking southward. The most significant political influence was that upon political thought in Puerto Rico.

The least important influence was the cultural. This was true due to the different background of the two peoples, the Old World training of most of the Puerto Rican editors, and the differences of language and religion. All of these prevented any more than the exchange of views between isolated men of letters. Cultural influences, before the days of the Good Neighbor Policy and countless good-will missions, were largely restricted to literary relationships. This, when the differences of language, history, tradition, and customs are taken into account, was a weak reed.

Northern publishing houses with their translation of American books into Spanish did much to reveal the American way to the Latin-American. The Yankee educational progress, the press, and individual Americans were admired, but little could be done to bring about closer connections between the United States and Puerto Rico as long as the Spanish government opposed it. The press voice of the Spanish authorities, the Boletín Mercantil, helped to counteract any American cultural infusion with its talk of Pan-Hispanism, lynchings, race-riots, and Indian massacres in the Model Republic.

The liberal press did its best to keep the discussion of the United States rationalistic and to prevent the main issue of political liberty from being clouded by sentiment. That press recognized the differences between the Anglo-Saxon and the Latin race; it discussed such topics as economic relations, democratic examples of both the individual American and his government, and Yankee foreign affairs in the light of liberalism, not imperialism.

The editors of the era, conservative and liberal, were men of talent, excellent education, and firm convictions. The liberals were willing to suffer governmental displeasure for criticizing Spanish policy in the Antilles. In the main their liberalism was consistent and did not abate with persecution. Liberal courage and consistency were proven by the reaction to the Componte and to the unjust trials of 1895. Rather than discouraging or vanquishing the liberals the persecutions had the opposite effect.

Liberal anti-American articles appear at times of disillusionment, as after the Commercial Treaty of 1892, or in periods of extreme pressure, as just before the Spanish-American War.

The Puerto Rican liberals demanded a more complete freedom than that granted by the Spanish colonial system, a freedom which was to be guaranteed by a definite pledge cn the part of the home government. The tangible result of this was the granting of a more liberal way of government in the form of the Sagasta Pact in 1897. Had Spain really been interested in the political well being of its insular subjects, it would have granted this reform long before American political theories were used by the liberals as weapons to fight reaction.

98

BIBLIOGRAPHY

Newspapers

Autonomista, El: San Juan. Periódico Político. A weekly paper, published
every Saturday. It called itself the official organ of the Autonomist
Party. As the name implies, it was dedicated to the ideal of autonomy
for Puerto Rico. Director: José Leoncio Rodríguez; Administrador:
Angel A. Mariani; Redactor-Jefe: Eloy de Ecenarro. First appeared
May 2, 1895.

Balanza, La: San Juan. Periódico político, mercantil, teatral, de literatura,
noticias y anuncios. A conservative paper. First published twice week-
ly; in 1893, three times weekly; in 1896, a daily. Director: Manuel M.
Marxuach; later the following men became editors: Alberto Régulez,
Manuel Tenés, J. Bengoechea; Redactores: Juan Pujol, J. Rodríguez
Arias. Administrador: Jacinto Anfosso; later, Salvador González
Fígueroa, Julián Bengoechea. The paper lasted for ten years, October
of 1887 to August of 1897. Since it first appeared during the year of the
Componte this fact is sufficient proof of its conservative character.

Bandera Española, La: San Juan. Dedicado al Ejército, Marina, Volun-
tarios de esta isla y de interés general. A conservative paper. Published weekly. First appeared in July, 1891; ceased publicatio. in 1897.
Director-Propietario: Emilio de Castaños; next it was directed by R.
López Landrón.

Boletín Instructivo y Mercantil de Puerto Rico (Boletín Mercantil): Organo
de los Españoles sin Condiciones. Published under the auspices of the
Junta de Comercio. Appeared twice weekly at first, later three times
weekly, and in the end it was a daily paper. This paper was the semi-
official organ of the Spanish government in Puerto Rico. It was the conservative paper, had the full support of the Spanish government, was
the most substantial of all the papers of the period from the point of
view of size, but was completely reactionary in all its policies. This
was the paper that declared 'even the air is Spanish'. Its editor was
one of the leaders of the Componte. Directores by periods: Ignacio
Guasp, 1844-1871; José Pérez Moris, 1871-1881; Díaz Caneja, 1881-
1898; A. Pineda, several months of 1898; Nemesio Pérez Moris, 1898-
1902; José Pérez Losada, 1902-1916; Luis Díaz Caneja, 1916-1918.
First appeared March 2, 1839; ceased publication at the end of 1918.

Bomba, La: Ponce. Organo del Pueblo. Published three times each week.
Fundador y Director: Evaristo Izcoa Díaz. Redactor: Rafael R. Muñoz.
Administrador: Zoilo Rodríguez. First epoch: from February 7 to
May 3, 1895. Second epoch: from September 22 to October 18, 1898.
The editor, Izcoa Díaz, was of the 'attack' type in journalism. To him
the government was wrong, whether that government was Spanish or
American. During the first epoch of the paper (its full life was seventeen numbers) the editor was placed in jail with the appearance of number ten of the paper. With that number (March 28, 1895) the paper continued under the direction of Rafael R. Muñoz. Izcoa Díaz' name still
appeared as editor but was followed by these words (en la carcel). The
paper was suspended during its second epoch by General Henry for an
article entitled "¿Bandidos o Soldados?"

Borinquen: New York City. Periódico Quincental, Organo de la Sección
Puerto Rico del Partido Revolucionario Cubano. Administrador y
Secretario de Redacción: Roberto H. Todd. Sr. Todd has had a long
and distinguished career in Puerto Rico. He was the mayor of the
capital, San Juan, for twenty years (not successively), the Commissioner of Immigration, 1921-1925, a Republican National Committeeman of
Puerto Rico, Secretary of the Puerto Rico Section of the Cuban Revolutionary Party, 1895-1898, and at present is Executive Secretary of the
Puerto Rican Bar Association.

Buscapié, El: San Juan. Periódico para todos. Director-propietario:
Manuel Fernández Juncos. Annalist: Abelardo Morales Ferrer; redactores: José Pablo Morales, Matías Gonzáles Garcia. The first number of the paper appeared April 1, 1877 as a weekly. In October of 1893
it began to publish two numbers each week. The last number of the
paper appeared on June 25, 1899. There was a brief second epoch from
October 17, 1917, to June 29, 1918. It was mainly a satirical paper. It
did much to further literary development in the island. Much space was
given to folklore, Puerto Rican customs, and the theater. The editor
had a complete command of satire, irony, and humor and was one editor
who could discuss politics and make people laugh over them. The conservative papers were afraid of his style of writing and, consequently,
said little against him. It could be classified as a liberal paper.

Clamor del País, El: Periódico autonomista. San Juan. The paper was
devoted to liberal reform and autonomy. It appeared three times each
week. Director: Julián E. Blanco, in 1884; next came Salvador Brau
and Francisco Díaz (interim). Administrador-Gerente: Arturo Córdova.
Propietario: José T. Silva (next was Salvador Brau). First appeared
May 15, 1883; ceased publication in 1894. This paper and its great editor, Salvador Brau, was highly respected by the Spanish government.
Brau, according to the general consensus, was the best historian of
the nineteenth century in Puerto Rico. He was excellent as a socio-
logist, good as a dramatist and a poet, but was best as a prose writer.
He was a strong liberal, sincere, but, unfortunately, unrecognized by
twentieth century Puerto Rico.

Concordia, La: Lares. Periódical liberal. Fundador-Director: Vicente
Viñas Martínez. Administrador: Vicente Borges Ortiz. Colaboradores:
José Vidal Cardona, Dr. Manuel Saldaña, Juan Gregorio Ramos. It first
appeared in June, 1897, and lasted only for several months.

Correspondencia de Puerto Rico, La: San Juan. Diario absolutamente im-
parcial, eco de la opinión y de la prensa. Fundador-Director: Ramón
B. López. Directores in various epochs: Francisco Ortea, Dr. M. Zeno
Gandía, Juan Braschi, Joaquín Barreiro, Luis Cuevas Zequeira, Conrado
Asenjo, Enrique Colón-Baerga, Fernando Sierra Berdecía, Emilio R.
Delgado, Francisco M. Zeno. Founded on December 18, 1890 and is
still in existence. It is the oldest daily paper in existence in Puerto Rico.

Democracia, La: Ponce, Caguas, San Juan. Trisemanario político. Later
it became a daily paper beginning with May 1, 1893. It was the organ of
the Autonomist Party. Fundador y Director: Luis Muñoz Rivera. It had
three epochs. They were: (1) Ponce; July 1, 1890, was the date of the
first publication. Appeared three times each week until 1893 when it
became an afternoon daily. (2) Caguas: established in that city in 1900;
remained there until 1904. (3) San Juan; its first number appeared in
San Juan on June 1, 1904. The paper is still in existence as a daily paper.

Diario de Puerto Rico: San Juan. (De avisos y noticias; de carácter católico). It has the appearance of a trade paper more than anything else. Director: Eugenio de Jesús López Gaztambide. Appeared in September of 1896. Short lived.

Diario de Puerto Rico, El: San Juan. Periódico popular de la tarde. Redactores: Manuel Fernández Juncos, Manuel F. Rossy, Francisco del Valle Atiles, Luis Sánchez Morales, José Gordils, José A. Daubón, Ezequiel Martínez Quintero, Abelardo Morales Ferrer, Guillermo Power. Administrador: Arturo Córdova. It first appeared July 6, 1893 and seems to have gone out of existence about July 15, 1894. It was published daily, including Sundays.

Eco, El: Yauco. Periódico bisemanal. Defensor de los intereses generales del país y los particulares de la localidad. Fundador: José G. Torres. Redactor: Modesto Cordero. Administrador: Heraclio Vázquez Arroyo, Pelegrin López de Victoria. First appeared November 3, 1895; ceased publication November 1, 1896. This paper gave most of its attention to local affairs, especially to the future of coffee in Puerto Rico.

Ecos del Manglar: Cataño. Semanario no Político, de Literatura y Anuncios. Published every Sunday. Director: Romualdo Vallés. First appeared March 24, 1895; lasted one month; disappeared in April, 1895.

Estudio, El: Ponce. Periódico de Propaganda, y eco del movimiento general del Libre-pensamiento. Director: Andrés Corazón González. Redactores y Colaboradores: Manuel Zeno Gandía, Rafael Muñoz, Carlos Toro Fernández, T. Carrión Maduro. Administrador-Gerente: José Morín Fernández. First appeared on May 2, 1892. Ceased publication in May of 1893. Re-appeared in July of 1893; disappeared in December of 1893.

Gaceta de Puerto Rico, La: San Juan. (Periódico oficial del gobierno. El primero que se publicó en Puerto Rico. Salía los miércoles y sábados). There is some doubt as to the exact date of its foundation. It is certain that it first appeared in 1806, 1807, or 1808 but there is no concrete proof to support any one of those dates as being the correct one. It began daily publication in 1823. The next change came on November 5, 1898, with General Order Number 10 (U.S. sovereignty) when it was declared Gaceta Oficial del Gobierno de Puerto Rico. It ceased publication in September, 1902. During the period 1888-1898 the paper had no news value other than court announcements, trials, and the activities of the Guardia Civil. It was purely a governmental announcement sheet by 1888.

Instrucción Pública, La: San Juan. Revista semanal, dedicada al fomento de la instrucción y a la defensa de los intereses del magisterio. It was the organ of the Teachers' Association of Puerto Rico and of the Directory of the Association of Women whose purpose was a more complete education of Puerto Rican women. It was a school paper, the best one that the people of Puerto Rico had in that respect. Abelardo González Font edited the paper but the articles were written by some one else. However, he had all the responsibility for those articles before the censors. This man was not a teacher by profession. The paper was a business venture. Nevertheless, it offered the above mentioned associations a means of expression which it could otherwise not have had.

It was primarily a school paper, abstained from politics, and was the best paper of its kind in Puerto Rico. Published every Sunday. Directores propietarios: González & Co. First appeared in February, 1881, and lasted about ten years.

Integridad Nacional, La: San Juan. Periódico Político, Científico, Literario, de Noticias y Anuncios. Defensor de los intereses generales de España en América. Interprete de las aspiraciones del Partido Incondicionalmente Español. This paper was as rabid as the Boletín Mercantil in its defense of Spain. Its main editor, Vicente Balbás, was a Puerto Rican and a son of a man who had been prominent in 1887 during the Componte. Vicente Balbás was the only Puerto Rican prosecuted by the U.S. Government during the First World War for his attacks on the draft. He was sentenced to Atlanta but was pardoned by President Wilson. After 1898 he became the editor of the Heraldo Español. The editorials of this paper dealt with educational reforms, attacks upon co-education, and the teaching of English in Puerto Rico. La Integridad Nacional first appeared in 1885, failed, and re-appeared in December of 1888. It ceased publication in 1898.

Látigo, El: Aguadilla. Periódico político español. A weekly paper. Director, Redactor and Administrador: Emilio de Mazarredo. First appeared in June of 1895; disappeared in August of 1896.

Liberal, El: San Juan. A daily paper. It originated as a result of the Sagasta Pact; the object of the paper was to promote a greater understanding between the Liberals of Madrid and those of Puerto Rico who were united by the Sagasta Pact. It was the organ of the Autonomist group of Luis Muñoz Rivera. That group was known as the 'Grupo Autonomista Liberal'. Founder of the paper: Luis Muñoz Rivera. Director: Rosendo Rivera Colón. Administrador: Juan Escudero Miranda. Redactores: Luis Rodríguez Cabrero, Sergio Cuevas Zequeira. First appeared on January 10, 1898; ceased publication about July 8, 1898.

Libertad, La: Ponce. Ciencias, Literatura. Noticias, Anuncios. Published three times weekly. Director-Fundador: Félix Matos Bernier. Colaboradores y Redactores: Rosendo Rivera Colón, Francisco R. Montañez, José Pico Matos, Juan P. Terreforte, Germán Vega. Administrador: Arturo Idrach (later Francisco E. Montañez). First appeared on February 18, 1894. Due to trouble with the authorities Bernier changed the name of the paper to El Cautivo on April 23, 1896 and temporarily withdrew from the staff. La Libertad resumed publication as a daily on August 8, 1895. Suspended publication again, briefly, returned on March 4, 1896, and continued until its final fall on July 28, 1897. Félix Matos Bernier was a good writer, a poet, and a prominent leader in the Autonomist movement but no radical.

Magisterio de Puerto Rico, El: San Juan. Revista profesional de instrucción pública, órgano de todos los centros de enseñanza de la isla. Published every Sunday. Director: Alberto Régulez y Sanz del Río. Administrador: José F. Díaz. First appeared January 6, 1889. The editor was a Spaniard, a good writer, the author of several Latin and rhetoric texts for high school, and the Director of the Instituto Civil, 1885-1886.

Mentor, El: San Juan. Órgano de la enseñanza. Published on the fifth, fifteenth, and twenty-fifth of each month. Director: José Leoncio Rodríguez; in 1895 J. E. Martínez Quintero. Administrador: Pedro C. Timothée. First appeared August 5, 1893.

Momio, El: San Juan. Semanario político, satírico, independiente. Published every Sunday. Director: Antonio Salgado. Administrador: Ramón Llovet. The next editor was Ramón Correa. First appeared August 1, 1897; disappeared at the end of 1898.

Nación Española, La: San Juan. Órgano del Partido Español Incondicional. Motto of the paper: "The triumph of reason is in justice and law". Appeared twice weekly. The paper claimed to be politically independent but it inclined to the conservative side. Director: José Joaquín Ribó; others in the paper: Ignacio Guasp, Francisco Valderrama, José Arnau Igarávidez, Arturo Guasp. First appeared in December of 1882; disappeared in July of 1892.

País, El: San Juan. Diario autonomista. Director: J. E. Martínez Quintero. From December 4, 1895 it appeared without an editor but in reality there were two, D. Enrique C. Hernández and Nosé C. Rossy. Colaborators: José Celso Barbosa, J. Gómez Brioso, M. F. Rossy, José Gordils, F. Amy, Cruz Castro. Administrador: Luis Berríos Borges. First appeared August 7, 1895; disappeared in 1902. This paper was one of the leading Autonomist organs. After the Sagasta Pact the paper became the organ of the orthodox Autonomists whose principle remained that of no alliance with Spanish political parties. That was the point of difference between the group of Luis Muñoz Rivera and that of José Celso Barbosa. The former party leader believed that reform could come quicker through alliance with the Spanish Liberal party---hence Louis Muñoz Rivera's work in favor of the Sagasta Pact.

Palenque de la Juventud, El: San Juan. This was the first paper edited for young people. Director: M. Quevedo Báez. Colaborators: Luis Sánchez Morales, Pedro de Angelis, Mariano Abril, José Gordils, Ferdinand R. Cestero, J. A. Negrón Sanjurjo, A. Contreras Ramos, Salvador Canals. Administrador: Pedro de Angelis. First appeared in January of 1886; failed and reappeared in October of 1888 which marked its second epoch.

Pequeña Antilla, La: Ponce. Trisemanario político de asuntos útiles al procomún, literatura, ciencias, artes y anuncios. Director: Luis Caballer (later Pedro Bayonet). Redactores y Colaboradores: L. A. Ponce de León, Tomás Carrión Maduro, Federico Matos Bernier, Rosendo Rivera Colón, Agustín Navarrete, Carlos del Toro Fernández. First appeared on November 23, 1895; disappeared July 28, 1898. The real leader of the paper was Luis Caballer, an upright and honest newspaper man who, because of his intransigent liberalism, was much persecuted by the Spanish authorities.

Pequeño Diario, El: Arecibo. Antes "La Voz de la Montaña". Diario popular completamente imparcial e independiente. Director: Manuel de J. Gorbea Guzmán. Administrador: Elías Montalvo Colberg. First appeared in March of 1895; ceased publication for a time and then reappeared in August of 1895. Suspended by the American military government at the end of 1898 when it began to publish in Mayagüez.

Razón, La: Mayagüez. Órgano del Partido Autonomista. Published three times each week. The second paper by this name in Mayagüez; the first was established in 1870 by José Ramón Freyre and ceased publication at the end of 1874. The second La Razón first appeared January 23, 1890 and ceased publication in July of 1891. Director-Propietario: Mario Braschi. Administrador: Francisco Llavat. Redactores: Francisco Ortea, Magín Raldiris. Mario Braschi was an excellent writer, a sincere liberal, and extremely persona non grata to the Spanish authorities.

República, La: Arecibo. Periódico Liberal. Published twice each week. Director: José de Diego. Redactor: (and next editor) Rosendo Rivera Colón. Administrador: Augustín Combell. First appeared January 19, 1893. Ceased publication 'temporarily' in July of 1893.

Revista Mercantil, La: Ponce. Director: Luis R. Velázquez. The paper called itself 'Defensor de los intereses Generales del País'; it was mainly a commercial organ. It was published three times each week. First appeared April 18, 1892 and went out of existence some time in 1897.

Revista Puertorriqueña: San Juan. Letras, Ciencias, Artes. A monthly paper. Director and founder: Manuel Fernández Juncos. Colaboradores: J. P. Morales, Brau, Zeno Gandía, Ferrer, Daubón, Gordils, Coll y Toste and some other of the best writers of Puerto Rico. It first appeared at the end of 1887; ceased publication in 1893. There are seven volumes in all. This publication afforded a means of expression to a group of writers who formed a golden age in Puerto Rican literature; without the Revista Puertorriqueña many articles by those men would have irretrievably been lost.

Revista Blanca, La: Mayagüez. (First epoch) A weekly paper. It called itself 'Semanario de literatura, ciencias, artes. Dedicado especialmente al bello sexo'. Director: José E. González Quiara (later Mariano R. Palmer). Redactor: Eugenio Astol. Administrador: Adriano T. López. Colaboradores: Manuel Ma. Sama, Carlos Casanovas, José de J. Domínguez. First appeared July 12, 1896. Disappeared in 1902. When Mariano R. Palmer became the editor the paper was known as La Revista Blanca, Periódico Literario y Artístico.

Revista de Agricultura, Industria y Comercio: San Juan. Published on the tenth of every month. Dedicated to the development of the resources of Puerto Rico in a more scientific manner. Fundador: Federico Asenjo. Administrador: Domingo Ramírez Soto. Redactores y Colaboradores: J. J. Acosta, Agustín Stahl, Tulio Larrinaga, Santiago Mac Cormick, Calixto Romero, Aureliano Jiménez, León Acuña y Angel Basconi. First appeared June 9, 1885; ceased publication in 1895.

Reforma Agricola, La: San Juan. Órgano de la Asociación de Agricultores. Director: Julián E. Blanco. Redactor-Jefe: Fernando López Tuero. First appeared September 21, 1893. Published intermittently until 1897 when it is thought to have gone out of publication.

104

Books pertinent to the period

Acosta, José J.: Almanaque de la Isla de Puerto Rico. San Juan; Publicado por la "Revista de Agricultura, Industria, y Comercio"; 1890, 1893, 1897.

Abril, Mariano: Sensaciones de un Cronista. San Juan; Tip. de "La Democracia"; 1903.

Adams, Randolph Greenfield: History of the Foreign Policy of the United States. New York; The Macmillan Co.; 1924.

Amy, Francisco J.: Predicar en Desierto. San Juan; Tip. "El Alba"; 1907.
    A series of articles that Amy wrote in various papers. He desired a closer co-operation between the Americans and the Puerto Ricans. He himself was a product of Americanization.

Anonymous: Puerto Rico por dentro; Cartas Abiertas; julio y agosto   *
de 1888. Madrid; Imp. de José Gil y Navarro; 1888.

Arrillaga Roqué, Juan: Memorias de Antaño; Historia de de un viaje á   *
España.
    Arrillaga went to Spain in 1887 to inform the Spanish government about the Componte. He was largely responsible for the removal of the governor and the ending of the Componte.

Bleyer, Willard Grosvenor: Main Currents in the History of American Journalism. New York; Houghton Mifflin Co.; 1927.

Busquets, Ernesto: Páginas altruistas. Mayagüez; Tip. "Unión Obrera"; 1908.

Bonafoux, Luis: Ultramarinos. Madrid; Imp. de M. Tello; 1882.

Balbás Capó, Vicente: Puerto Rico á los diaz años de Americanizatión. San Juan; Tip. "Heraldo Español"; 1910.
    This book is a strong criticism of the American occupation of Puerto Rico by an unreconstructed 'incondicional'.

Balbás, Casiano: El Partido Incondicionalmente Español de Puerto   *
Rico. San Juan; Tip. del "Boletín Mercantil"; 1887.
    A series of editorial articles published in La Integridad Nacional by Balbas explaining the views of the conservative party in Puerto Rico.

Ballesteno Muñoz, José: Guia Comercial y Agricola de Puerto Rico.   *
Mayagüez; 1890.

Barbosa, José Celso: La Obra de José Celso Barbosa. San Juan; Imp. Venezuela; 1937. 4 vols.

Blanco Fernández, Antonio: España y Puerto Rico, 1820-1930. San Juan; Tip. Cantero Fernández; 1930.
    A series of articles on literature, economics, and history. Conservative.

Blanch, José: Directorio Comercial é Industrial de la Isla de Puerto Rico para 1894. San Juan; Tip. de "La Correspondencia"; 1894.

Blanco, Tomas: Prontuario Historica de Puerto Rico. Madrid; Imp. de Juan Pueyo; 1935.
History of Puerto Rico during the colonial period up to 1898.

Bona, Félix de: Cuba, Santo Domingo, y Puerto Rico. Madrid; Imp. de Manuel Galiano; 1861.
A comparative study of the three Antilles; it discusses the idea of a confederation of the Antilles from an economic point of view primarily.

Brau, Salvador: Ecos de la Batalla; artículos periodísticos. San Juan; Imp. de José Gonzalez Font; 1886.
A debate with the conservative papers. It shows his admiration for the American democracy which he thought could well be implanted in Puerto Rico.

Brau, Salvador: Historia de Puerto Rico. New York; D. Appleton & Co.; 1904.

Cabotaje con la Peninsula y el Tratado de Comercio con los los Estados-Unidos de la América del Norte, El. San Juan; Imp. de Gobierno; 1891.

Carroll, Henry K.: Report on the Island of Porto Rico. (U.S. Treasury Department, Document Number 2118) Washington; Government Printing Office; 1899.
A report on the population, civil government, commerce, industries, products, roads, tariffs, and currency of Puerto Rico. Carroll was sent to Puerto Rico by President McKinley.

Castañer Casanovas, Pedro: La crisis política y economica de Puerto Rico. Aguadilla; Tipografía "El Criollo"; 1909.

Castellano, Tomas: Canje de la Moneda en Puerto Rico. Madrid; Imp. de los Hijos de J. A. Garcia; 1896.

Celis Aguilera, José de: Mi Grano de Arena para la historia política de Puerto Rico. San Juan; Imp. de Acosta; 1886.
History of the various political parties and of autonomy for Puerto Rico. It tells much of his personal labors in politics.

Chadwick, F. E.: The Relations of the United States and Spain. New York; Charles Scribner's Sons; 1909.

Coll Cuchi, Cayetano: Notas Políticas. San Juan; Tip. "Boletín Mercantil"; 1909.

Coll y Toste, Cayetano: Historia de la Instrucción Pública en Puerto Rico hasta el año 1898. San Juan; Talleres Tipograficos "Boletín Mercantil"; 1910.

Coll y Toste, Cayetano: Boletín Histórico de Puerto Rico; Publicación bimestral. San Juan; Tip. Cantero, Fernández y Co.; 1914-1927. 14 vols.

Colón, E. E.: Datos sobre la Agricultura de Puerto Rico antes de 1898. San Juan; Tip. Cantero; 1930.
Written by a man acquainted with his subject. Colón was formerly a Commissioner of Agriculture in Puerto Rico.

Constitución Autonómica, Político, Administrativo de las islas de Cuba y Puerto Rico. San Juan; Sucesión de José J. Acosta; 1897.

Cruz Monclova, Lidio: Historia Política de Puerto Rico en el Siglo XIX (MSS).
When printed this book will be the definitive work on the political history of Puerto Rico during the nineteenth century. It is written by a scholar who is deeply conscientious and fully acquainted with historical method.

Cummings, A. J.: The Press and a Changing Civilization. London; John Lane, The Bodley Head; 1936.

Dalmau Ganet, Sebastián: Luis Muñoz Rivera. San Juan; Tip. "Boletín Mercantil"; 1917.

Dauban, José Antonio: Cosas de Puerto Rico. San Juan; Tip. "La Corre- * spondencia"; 1904.

Deschamps, Eugenio: Juan Morel Campos. Ponce; Tip. "El Correo de * Puerto Rico"; 1899.

Desmond, Robert W.: The Press and World Affairs. New York; D. Appleton-Century Co.; 1937.

Díaz Caneja, Ignacio: Waterloo Político. San Juan; Tip. del "Boletín Mercantil"; 1891.
The author entitles it a critical examination of the modern political theories. This man was the editor of the Boletín Mercantil, the most reactionary of all Puerto Rican newspapers; naturally his criticism would be of the conservative order.

Díaz Caneja, Ignacio: Las Reformas del Sr. Maura. San Juan; Tip. del "Boletín Mercantil"; 1893.

Díaz Caneja, Ignacio: La Autonómia de las Antillas. San Juan; Imprenta * del "Boletín Mercantil"; 1887.
This book gives the history, principles, errors, tendencies, and future of autonomy from the point of view of an arch-conservative.

Elzaburu, Manuel: El Sentimiento de Nacionalidad. San Juan; Imp. Gonzalez Font; 1889.

Foreign Commerce of Cuba, Porto Rico, Hawaii, The Philippines, and Samoan Islands. Their Imports and Exports by Countries; also the Commerce of the United States Therewith. (Bureau of Statistics) Washington; Treasury Department; 1899.

Fernández Juncos, Manuel: Habana y Nueva-York; Estudios de Viaje. San Juan; Biblioteca y Tipografía de "El Buscapié"; 1886.

Figueroa, S.: Ensayo Biográfico. Ponce; Tip. "El Vapor"; 1888.
A study, as the author puts it, "of those who have contributed the most to the progress of Puerto Rico".

Gómez, Juan Gualberto &
Sendras Y Burin, Antonio: La Isla de Puerto Rico. Madrid; Imp. de José Gil y Navarro; 1891.

Gramling, Oliver: AP, The Story of News. New York; Farrar & Rinehart, Inc.; 1940.

Hitchcock, Frank H.: Trade of Puerto Rico. Washington; United States Printing Office; 1898.

Irwin, Will: Propaganda and the News. New York; Whittlesey House; 1936.

Jesús, José de: La Autonómia Administrativa en Puerto Rico. Mayagüez; * Tip. Comercial; 1887.

Labra, Rafael María de: Aspecto internacional de la Cuestión de Cuba. Madrid; Tip. de Alfredo Alonso; 1900.

Labra, Rafael María de: La Autonomía Colonial en España. Madrid, Imp. de los sucesores de Cuesta; 1892.

Labra, Rafael María de: La política antillana en la metrópoli española. Madrid; Imp. de "El Liberal"; 1891.

Labra, Rafael María de: La Reforma electoral en las Antillas Españolas. Madrid; Imp. de "El Liberal"; 1891.

Labra, Rafael María de: La Reforma Política de Ultramar; Discursos y folletos, 1868-1901. Madrid; Tip. de Alfredo Alonso; 1901.

López Tuero, Fernando: Estudios de Economía Rural. San Juan; Imprenta del "Boletín Mercantil"; 1893.

López Tuero, Fernando: La Reforma Agrícola. San Juan; Imprenta del "Boletín Mercantil"; 1891.

Malaret, Augusto: Salvadro Brau. San Juan; Talleres tipográficos "Boletín Mercantil"; 1910.

Mariano Quiñones, Francisco: Historia de los Partidos reformista y conservador de Puerto Rico. Mayagüez; Tip. Comercial; 1889.

Mathews, John Mabry: American Foreign Relations. New York; D. Appleton-Century Co.; 1938.

Maymí Cruells, Francisco: ¿Canje tenemos? Crisis segura. San Juan; Sucesión de José J. Acosta; 1895.

Mayoral Barnes, Manuel: Anuario y Guia Completa de la Isla de Puerto Rico, 1494-1921. San Juan, 1921.

Messages and Papers of the Presidents. New York; Bureau of National Literature, Inc.; Vols. XI, XII, XIII.

Miller, Paul G.: Historia de Puerto Rico. New York; Rand McNally & Co.; 1922.

Mixer, Knowlton: Puerto Rico; History and Conditions. New York; The Macmillan Co.; 1926.

Montañez, Francisco E.: Granos de Arena, Colección de Artículos, políticos y literarios. Ponce; "El Telégrafo"; 1895.

Morales, José P.: Miscelanea. San Juan; Imp. Acosta; 1895.
    A collection of articles dealing with the history and economic and
social conditions of Puerto Rico.

Morales Cabrera, Pablo: Biografía de Román Baldorioty de Castro.
Bayamon; Tip. "El Progreso"; 1910.

Morales Miranda, José: Misceláneas Históricas. San Juan; Tip. "La
Correspondencia de Puerto Rico"; 1924.

Mullenhoff, Guillermo: Cuestión Monetaria. Mayagüez; Tip. Comercial;
1888.

Muñoz Morales, Luis: El Status Político de Puerto Rico. San Juan; Tip.
"El Compas"; 1921.
    The author gives various formulas for the eventual status of Puerto
Rico in which he favors a special treatment, half way between classical
statehood and the Canadian system.

Muñoz Rivera, Luis: Obras Completas de Luis Muñoz Rivera. Madrid;
Editorial Puerto Rico; 1925. 4 vols. Seleccionadas y recopiladas por
Luis Muñoz Marín.

Neumann Gandia, Eduardo: Benefactores y hombres notables de Puerto
Rico. Ponce; "La Libertad"; 1896, Vol. I). Ponce; "Listin Comercial";
1899, Vol. II. 2 vols.

Osuna, Juan José: Education in Porto Rico. New York; Columbia University
Press; 1923.

Partido Revolucionario Cubano: Memoria de los trabajos realizados por la
Sección Puerto Rico del Partido revolucionario Cubano, 1895-1898.
New York; Imprenta de A. W. Howes; 1900.

Pasarell, Emilio J.: Origen y Desarrollo de las Representaciones Teatrales
en Puerto Rico. (MSS).
    When completed this work will be the source on the development of
the theater in Puerto Rico. No other writer has explored the field as
fully as Mr. Pasarell.

Pedreira, Antonio S.: Un Hombre del Pueblo: José Celso Barbosa. San
Juan; Imp. Venezuela; 1937.

Pedreira, Antonio S.: Bibliografía Puertorriquena, 1493-1930. Madrid;
Imprenta de la Librería y Casa Editorial Hernando; 1932.

Pedreira, Antonio S.: El Año Terrible del '87. San Juan; Imprenta Puerto
Rico; 1937.

Pedreira, Antonio S.: El Periodismo en Puerto Rico. La Habana; Imp.
Úcar, García y Cía.; 1941.
    This work is invaluable for an understanding of newspaper develop-
ment in Puerto Rico. This dissertation would have been seriously ham-
pered had this work not been available. The author of the dissertation
is deeply indebted to the late Dr. Pedreira for this book. Any errors in
the comments on the press bibliography are those of the writer and not
of Dr. Pedreira.

Puerto Rico Ateneo: Gratitud y progreso. San Juan; Tip. "Boletín Mercantil"; 1908.

Rippy, J. Fred: Historical Evolution of Hispanic-America. New York; F. S. Crofts & Co.; 1940.

Rivero, Angel: Crónica de la Guerra Hispano-Americana. Madrid; Imp. de los sucesores de Rivadeneyra; 1922.

Robertson, William Spence: Hispanic-American Relations. New York; Oxford University Press; 1923.

Rowe, L. S.: The United States and Porto Rico. New York; Longmans, Green, & Co.; 1904.

Salmon, Lucy Maynard: The Newspaper and the Historian. New York; Oxford University Press; 1923.

Stuart, Graham Henry: Latin America and the United States. New York; D. Appleton-Century Co.; 1938.

Sendras y Burin, Antonio: Propaganda Reformista; un Nuevo Partido. Madrid; Imp. de Emilio Saco y Brey; 1887.
    This book tells of the antecedents, formation, and aspirations of the Autonomist party of Puerto Rico.

Soto, Juan B.: Causas y Consecuencias; antecedentes diplomaticos y efectos de la guerra hispano-americana. San Juan; "La Correspondencia de Puerto Rico"; 1922.

Tapia y Rivera, Alejandro: Mis Memorias. New York; De Laisne & Rossboro Inco.; 1927.
    The book is mostly a description of the social, economic, and political conditions of Puerto Rico during the latter half of the nineteenth century.

Todd, Roberto H.: La Invasión Americana. San Juan; Cantero Fernández y Co.; 1938.

Todd, Roberto H.: La Genesis de la Bandera Puertorriqueña. San Juan; Cantero Fernández & Co.; 1938.

Valle, José G. del: A través de diez años, 1897-1907. Barcelona; Tip. de Feliu y Susuanna; 1907.

Van Middeldyk, R. A.: The History of Puerto Rico from the Spanish Discovery to the American Occupation. New York; D. Appleton & Co.; 1903.

Vijande, Enrique: La Cuestión Monetaria en Puerto Rico. Madrid; Tip. de Manuel Ginés Hernandez; 1889.

Wilgus, Alva Curtis: Development of Hispanic-America. New York; Farrar & Rinehart, Inc.; 1941.

Wisan, Joseph E.: The Cuban Crisis as Reflected in the New York Press, 1895-1898. New York; Columbia University Press; 1934.

---

* The Emilio J. Pasarell Collection

THE PUERTO RICAN EXPERIENCE

An Arno Press Collection

Berle, Beatrice Bishop. **Eighty Puerto Rican Families in New York City:** Health and Disease Studied in Context. New Foreword by the author. 1958

Blanco, Tomas. **El Prejuicio Racial en Puerto Rico.** (Racial Prejudice in Puerto Rico). 1948

Carroll, Henry K. **Report on the Island of Porto Rico;** Its Population, Civil Government, Commerce, Industries, Productions, Roads, Tariff, and Currency, With Recommendations. 1899

Cebollero, Pedro A. **A School Language Policy for Puerto Rico.** 1945

Chiles, Paul Nelson. **The Puerto Rican Press Reaction to the United States, 1888-1898.** 1944

Clark, Victor S., et al. **Porto Rico and Its Problems.** 1930

Coll Cuchí, José. **Un Problema en América.** (The American Problem). 1944

Colon, Jesus. **A Puerto Rican in New York and Other Sketches.** 1961

Enamorado Cuesta, J[ose]. **Porto Rico, Past and Present:** The Island After Thirty Years of American Rule. A Book of Information, Written for the American Reading Public, in the Interest and for the Benefit of the People of Porto Rico. [1929]

Fernández Vanga, Epifanio. **El Idioma de Puerto Rico y El Idioma Escolar de Puerto Rico.** (Language and Language Policy in Puerto Rico). 1931

Fleagle, Fred K. **Social Problems in Porto Rico.** 1917

Friedrich, Carl J. **Puerto Rico: Middle Road to Freedom.** 1959

Gallardo, José M., editor. **Proceedings of [the] Conference on Education of Puerto Rican Children on the Mainland (October 18 to 21, 1970).** 1972

Geigel Polanco, Vicente. **Valores de Puerto Rico.** (Puerto Rican Leaders). 1943

Institute of Field Studies, Teachers College, Columbia University. **Public Education and the Future of Puerto Rico: A Curriculum Survey, 1948-1949.** 1950

Jaffe, A[bram] J., editor. **Puerto Rican Population of New York City.** 1954

New York [City]. Welfare Council. **Puerto Ricans in New York City:** The Report of the Committee on Puerto Ricans in New York City of the Welfare Council of New York City. 1948

Osuna, Juan José. **A History of Education in Puerto Rico.** 1949

Perloff, Harvey S. **Puerto Rico's Economic Future:** A Study in Planned Development. 1950

Puerto Rican Forum. **The Puerto Rican Community Development Project:** Un Proyecto Puertorriqueño de Ayuda Mutua Para El Desarrollo de la Comunidad. A Proposal For a Self-Help Project to Develop the Community by Strengthening the Family, Opening Opportunities for Youth and Making Full Use of Education. 1964

Puerto Ricans and Educational Opportunity. 1975

The Puerto Ricans: Migration and General Bibliography. 1975

Roberts, Lydia J. and Rosa Luisa Stefani. **Patterns of Living in Puerto Rican Families.** 1949

Rosario, José C[olombán]. **The Development of the Puerto Rican Jíbaro and His Present Attitude Towards Society.** 1935

Rowe, L[eo] S. **The United States and Porto Rico:** With Special Reference to the Problems Arising Out of Our Contact with the Spanish-American Civilization. 1904

Siegel, Arthur, Harold Orlans and Loyal Greer. **Puerto Ricans in Philadelphia:** A Study of Their Demographic Characteristics, Problems and Attitudes. 1954

[Tugwell, Rexford G.] **Puerto Rican Public Papers of R. G. Tugwell, Governor.** 1945

United States-Puerto Rico Commission on the Status of Puerto Rico. **Status of Puerto Rico:** Report of the United States-Puerto Rico Commission on the Status of Puerto Rico, August 1966. 1966

United States-Puerto Rico Commission on the Status of Puerto Rico. **Status of Puerto Rico:** Selected Background Studies Prepared for the United States-Puerto Rico Commission on the Status of Puerto Rico, 1966. 1966

United States Senate. Select Committee on Equal Educational Opportunity. **Equal Educational Opportunity for Puerto Rican Children (Part 8):** Hearings Before the Select Committee on Equal Educational Opportunity of the United States Senate. 91st Congress, 2nd Session, Washington, D. C., November 23, 24 and 25, 1970. 1970

Van Middeldyk, R. A. **The History of Puerto Rico:** From the Spanish Discovery to the American Occupation. 1903

Wakefield, Dan. **Island in the City:** The World of Spanish Harlem. 1959

White, Trumbull. **Puerto Rico and Its People.** 1938